OPERATION GRASSHOPPER

A HISTORY OF ARMY AVIATION IN COMBAT IN KOREA

by

DARIO POLITELLA

PUBLISHED, JUNE, 195

$4.95 p. p.

PLEASE SEND TWO TEAR SHEETS OF YOUR REVIEW

THE ROBERT R. LONGO CO., INC.
1318 BEAUMONT DRIVE
WICHITA 4, KANSAS, U. S. A.

FORM A-14

LIBRARY OF CONGRESS
Catalog Card Number 58-11435

First Printing: April, 1958

Printed in United States of America
by Printing Incorporated
Wichita, Kansas

Published by
The ROBERT R. LONGO Company, Inc.
1318 Beaumont Drive
Wichita 4, Kansas

OPERATION GRASSHOPPER

Dario Politella

Foreword by
General Mark W. Clark, U.S.A.

OPERATION GRASSHOPPER

by

Dario Politella

The story of Army Aviation in Korea

from aggression to armistice

With a FOREWORD by General Mark W. Clark
formerly Commander of the United Nations
Forces in the Far East

Illustrated by Dan V. Cavliere
and Robert R. Longo

Dust Jacket by Jo Kotula

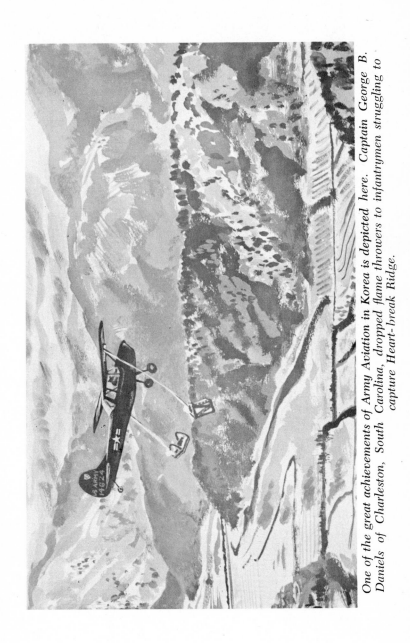

One of the great achievements of Army Aviation in Korea is depicted here. Captain George B. Daniels of Charleston, South Carolina, dropped flame throwers to infantrymen struggling to capture Heart-break Ridge.

TABLE OF CONTENTS

"American servicemen in future decades will owe a great debt to the dauntless pioneers of Army Aviation who learned their skills in World War II and developed them beyond all expectations on the bloody peninsula of Korea".

— General Mark W. Clark

FOREWORD

OPERATION GRASSHOPPER is the story of Army Aviation in Korea. It is a story that needs to be told, for in the extensive coverage of the Korean conflict there is little reference to this small, yet vital, segment of the Army. It helps to fill one of the many gaps in the military literature on the Korean war.

The book tells, among other things, how our Army pilots, flying light, unarmed planes, sought out and reported the movements of enemy forces, discovered Communist artillery positions and adjusted our destructive counter-battery fire, uncovered enemy troop concentrations, supply convoys, and other prime targets for the Air Force, and flew countless missions of mercy.

The author, Dario Politella, knows his subject. He served in Korea as a Public Information Officer for the Eighth Army. In that key spot he learned of the valorous deeds, frustrations, and problems of the pilots. Some may find it difficult to believe certain of the reported happenings, but I do not think that any who served in Korea will be found among them.

On other pages of this book there is recorded a message which I sent to Army Aviation on 6 June 1952 on the occasion of its tenth birthday. It was my privilege, as Commander of the United Nations Forces in the Far East, to tell the selfless men who comprised Army Aviation a little something of the esteem in which they were held. Thirteen months of additional bitter warfare only served to confirm what was said in that birthday message.

General Mark W. Clark, USA Ret.

PREFACE

This is the story of a silent service.

And it really begins at the end, rather than at the beginning, where most stories should start.

The end of this story begins at the climax of a decade, a golden decade during which a handful of Army men struggled to rear a somewhat illegitimate brainchild as one of the least-known members of the Army team. This is the story of Army Aviation operations in Korea which began during those hectic days when the ruddy skies through which they piloted their flimsy aircraft reflected the bloody campaigns of the out-manned and out-gunned United Nations troops fighting in the dark days of despair and frustration.

Army Aviation entered the Korea campaigns still as a paradox of terms as well as of fact. With air arms separated by their very nature from ground units, here was the exception to the rule. This was a service with split loyalties and dual training. Its flying members were simultaneously the glamorous fly-boys and the dog-faces of ground combat. Their jeeps were equipped with wings.

Army Aviation had been conceived during the Louisiana maneuvers of 1941 and delivered by the Army as an organic part of its family in 1942. The campaigns in Africa, Sicily, Italy, Normandy and in the Pacific had found Army Aviators in the forefront of action, but in the background of dispatches. The paradox of their existence had doomed them to obscurity because they formed an aviation unit of light aircraft flown by Army Officers who were carried on the rolls of ground units.

Yet, these unarmed and unarmored aircraft of Army Aviation had also trod the carpets of enemy flak so dramatically romanticized by the Air Force. They had also staggered back to their front-line bases literally on a wing and a prayer. And during their combat missions, they had directed the firing of more demolitions in a single hour of flying than had been dropped by whole squadrons of Flying Fortresses on hours-long missions.

Still, these miniature juggernauts of war had started out as fabric-covered metal and wood frames propelled through the air by engines generating less horsepower than the average family automobile. Their pilots had often joked that a sharpening of their skills was best accomplished by applying sandpaper to their buttocks.

The "Grasshoppers" were christened, so the story goes, at Camp Forrest, Tennessee, in November 1941 during Army maneuvers. In the midst of a mock battle, Major General Ennis P. Swift, commander of the 1st Cavalry Division, is said to have called for "those grasshoppers" in requesting the spotting planes assigned to his Division. The name stuck.

For the early "Grasshoppers", all flying was by feel. Flight instruments of any consequence were neither supplied nor required. A compass and a fuel gauge, a tachometer and an oil pressure indicator were their only luxuries beyond an ingrained love for flying.

When the war broke out in Korea in 1950, a handful of Army Aviators in the theater found themselves equipped with the same aircraft of World War II and plagued by the same techniques of "field expedients" which had dictated their successful operations almost a decade before. They mustered every available "flying jeep" and went to war. Their missions were identical. Only the time, the place and the enemy were changed.

Hampered by lack of supplies, replacement parts and by their war-weary aircraft, these Army Aviators were able to write a creditable chapter in the history of military operations. Their efforts were lauded on 6 June 1952, the tenth anniversary of Army Aviation, when General Mark W. Clark, commander of the United Nations forces in the Far East, wrote:

> "I have followed with a great deal of interest the progress which this unique part of the Army team has made during the last decade. The faith which has nurtured and developed this arm has been justified in Korea. The very few men devoted to such service have accomplished so much through their courage, tenacity, and fighting efficiency that Army Aviation is one of the brightest spots in the bitter war being fought by the United Nations command

in Korea. Their efforts on missions of both tactical urgency and compassionate necessity have been magnificent. American servicemen in future decades will owe a great debt to the dauntless pioneers of Army Aviation who learned their skills in World War II and developed them beyond all expectations on the bloody peninsula of Korea. "

The same day, General James A. Van Fleet, commander of the Eighth United States Army Korea, wrote:

"Nowhere are the achievements of Army Aviation more keenly appreciated than among members of the Eighth Army. Against a numerically stronger enemy, Eighth Army has upheld the finest traditions of American arms with a combination of superior equipment, skill and courage. Army Aviation in Korea has provided a magnificent example of the effectiveness of that combination. . . "

President Dwight D. Eisenhower, on a visit to Korea on 3 December 1952, prior to assuming office was so impressed with the efficiency of the Army Aviation mission that he wrote:

"Some of my staff tell me that we flew almost three hundred miles with you (Lt. Col. J. Elmore Swenson, EUSAK Aviation Officer) and your pilots during the visit to Korea.

"I must say that I have never seen transportation handled so rapidly and efficiently on a troop visit. I know it took a lot of careful planning on your part, and I would like to express to you and to all the members of your command my deep appreciation for such outstanding service. . . "

These plaudits of necessity speak of the Army Aviators as a group of highly trained volunteers who played their parts as the unsung heroes of ground combat in Korea. OPERATION GRASSHOPPER tells the stories of the individuals who, by their daring in day to day flying, helped to form the big picture of Army Aviation operations.

The author hopes that by this telling, Army Aviation may be a silent service no longer.

Dario Politella

ACKNOWLEDGMENTS

The story of Army Aviation contained in this volume results from a frustrating search for material through two years of constant effort. Few records are available because the Army Aviation role in the Korea operations has been over-shadowed by the more glamorous achievements of the Air Force and the greater public sympathy for the story of the GI in the foxhole. Even official records are lacking because Army Aviation operations for the most part have been integrated so deeply into historical resumes as one more anonymous contribution to the battle reports that they may well be obscured for all time.

Most of the material recounted here, therefore, has been gathered from the recollections of Army Aviators who actually lived them. OPERATION GRASSHOPPER could not have been written without the assistance of Captain E. M. Lynch, who had been engaged in Army Aviation operations in Korea during the first months of hostilities, and Lt. Col. J. Elmore Swenson, who made significant contributions to the Army Aviation activities in Korea during 19 months of service as aviation officer, Eighth United States Army in Korea. Through their efforts, information from official records and personal diaries have been made available. And through their invaluable assistance, other flyers serving in Korea were contacted and their memories drained of pertinent recollections.

All of the information which appears as the history for the 1952 operations has been supplied by the author from copious notes taken in Korea while serving as information officer for the Army Aviation section, EUSAK. And throughout the book, the evaluations of the operations are those of the author and do not necessarily reflect the opinions of any of the individuals who assisted in making this book possible.

No book can be the result of a single effort. The author acknowledges the contributions of Lt. Col. Claude L. Shepard, formerly of the Career Management Division, Department of the Army; Lt. Col. Robert Hamilton, formerly director of training, the Army Aviation School, Fort Sill, Oklahoma; Major Francis X. Burgasser, formerly with the office of the Chief of Information, United States Army; Lt. Col. Raymond R. Evers, and Major Bruce O. Ihlenfeldt.

Capt. Arthur H. Kesten, editor of ARMY AVIATION magazine, Westport, Connecticut, has done yeoman service in the promotion of the OPERATION GRASSHOPPER project which resulted in gaining contacts with valuable sources of information. And credit is given here also to Ronald Moscati of Niagara Falls, New York, for his willing assistance in preparing photographs.

Several of the stories appearing in the book were published earlier in magazines. Acknowledgment is made to the editors of Air Facts, VFW Magazine, and Army Aviation for their kind permission to reproduce them here.

The author's thanks go also to the hundreds of pilots, observers, mechanics and crewmen whose deeds have made OPERATION GRASSHOPPER worth the telling.

CHAPTER 1

PRELUDE

TO WAR

During World War II, about 3,000 Army artillery officers were trained to man the light, unarmed and unarmored aircraft which they flew against the enemy in Europe and in the Pacific. Their combat missions were almost entirely restricted to reconnaissance of enemy movements and the adjustment of artillery firing.

With the coming of V-J Day and the wholesale return of servicemen to civilian life, only a handful of these flyers remained on active duty with the Army. During the post-war years, these men were responsible for a continuing development of light aircraft as established components of the Army team. Their tandem-seating, fabric-covered aircraft became obsolete as plans developed for all-metal, multi-passenger, higher-powered planes to take on more and more missions for the Army.

The Piper Cub L-4, that 65-horsepower, fabric-covered airplane which had given yeoman's service for almost a decade, was relegated to the sidelines of Army Aviation interest as plans for bigger and better planes took shape on the drawing boards. Even the Stinson Sentinel L-5, with its 185-horsepower engine, became obsolete. The all-metal Navion L-17 was purchased for courier and administrative missions. The Cub was succeeded by the L-16, a military version of the Aeronca Champion. But its only advantages were a slightly faster cruising speed and an injection-type carburetor which relieved the "Grasshopper" pilot of his cockpit concern for carburetor icing.

To expand the mission of Army Aviation, pilot training was opened to officers of every arm and some of the services of the ground forces. Missions graduated from the original artillery spotting for which Army Aviation had been designed to the support of Armor, Infantry, Corps of Engineers, Signal Corps and Ordnance.

Some experimentation with helicopters as battlefield vehicles was conducted. But the greatest attention of the Army Aviation planners was focused toward the development of new fixed-wing aircraft which would permit longer-range flights in greater comfort and at increased speeds. The peactime planners were also taking into consideration the difficulties of maintaining aircraft in the field, as well as of the need for a versatile aircraft which could be operated under every condition of terrain and climate.

But, in spite of all the planning and the dreaming of the pioneers of Army Aviation during these post-war years, Korea caught them with their flaps down. For when Korea became a household by-word in June 1950, Army Aviation was thrown into the conflict with the obsolete equipment of World War II.

The Korea campaigns had found Army Aviation in the middle of one of the difficult transition periods of development which have plagued the Army during peacetime. By 1950, the L-5 and L-16 aircraft had become obsolete and weary and unsuitable for operations in a rugged terrain. Despite the lesons of World War II, Army Aviators were still handicapped by out-moded communications systems, inefficient supply channels and inter-service jealousies.

Another problem confronting Army Aviation at the outbreak of the war was the shortage of pilot personnel. In spite of the existence of nearly 5,000 pilots who had been trained during the Second World War and after, only about 1,400 were within reach for immediate military service on the Army's stations already scattered around the world. Of these, fewer than 100 were available for combat missions during the first weeks of the fighting in Korea.

Under-manned and ill-equipped as it was, Army Aviation was called to participate in military campaigns which were to provide a stirring climax to less than a decade of development. In addition to the vicious enemy, the scene of battle was to provide the challenges of terrain and weather to make the second war in Army Aviation history a three-front action.

Although the topography of Korea was loosely termed mountainous, the real hazard in lightplane flying on that peninsula was not to be the height of the terrain masses; rather was it to be the frequency with which the hills appeared. Where one hill ended, another began in almost unending series. These jagged peaks rose from rice paddies which were terraced in the valleys. There was little relief from this succession of hills. Emergency landing areas were few and far between. Even the roads provided little respite from the monotony of hill upon hill and the perforation of the rice paddies. For the roads snaked and climbed their way at the pleasure of the hills, while only the sandy beds of the rivers were available for emergency landings, and these only during the dry seasons.

At the outset, it became obvious that the legend of the "postage stamp airforce" would have to be revised. During World War II, the "Grasshopper" pilots had earned their names and their reputations for the ease with which they could hop from pasture to pasture as they maintained close contact with the ground units for which they provided an elevated observation post. It was thought they could land anywhere. For in Europe and Africa particularly, the Cubs utilized to advantage the flat terrain and existing roads. But Korea changed all this. Engineers had to be called in to bulldoze airstrips from the rice paddies before efficient operations could begin.

The weather joined forces with the terrain to provide a further obstacle to lightplane operations. Low ceilings and restricted visibilities forced the planes into the valleys where closed canyons and high-tension lines added to the hazards of flying. Fickle wind currents among the hills toyed with the skills of the pilots as they were buffeted over the bleak countryside. The changeable weather was as unpredictable as the front lines during those early days. And Will Rogers' axiom of Oklahoma weather was recalled: "If you don't like the weather now, wait five minutes -- it'll change".

Most of the flying in Korea was done under Visual Flight Rules, even at the risk of being dubbed "fair weather pilots" by the more daring, higher-flying Air Force pilots. And when the L-19 later offered VHF radio facilities and an instrument flight panel, keeping sight of the ground during flights proved the discretion of the pilots. Instrument flight facilities did not become available to the Army Aviators who could use them until later in the war. As a result, the Army flyers confined their flight paths to contact with the ground because of the rugged terrain features and the continuous guerrilla activities. If his engine failed while flying above the clouds, the only recourse to the pilot would be to bail out, rather than to take the risk of denting the side of a mountain.

Flying the highways in Korea proved to be the flyers' insurance against becoming lost. The magnetic compass came to have questionable value among the metal-storing mountains because in some areas the compass had a reported

deviation of as much as 15 degrees. Another important reason for flying along the roads was that they were the only
traveled routes where flyers could be helped in the event of
a forced landing. Planes crashing in the hills even a few
miles from the MSR (main supply route) in some areas
would never be found. And even after the second anniversary
of the fighting, flyers in the rear areas were ordered armed
during every flight because of UN-hunting guerrillas who
were scattered throughout the peninsula. A third reason
for hugging the MSR was that the road usually had been routed
along the topographical line of least resistance. Near it
were usually found the only places where safe forced landings
could be made.

When a plane on a cleared flight became lost, the searching
planes began their rescue operations along the MSR as a
matter of procedure. Pilots became convinced, therefore,
that the MSR was the best airway to follow.

Prominent rivers offered good navigational guides in addition
to the fact that during low-water seasons of the year, their
sandy edges made firm landing areas for distressed aircraft.
Here they could be repaired and flown out without much
"sweat."

If the geography of Korea provided few comforts for flyers,
ground travelers were even more unhappy. Flying by lightplane in Korea became the lesser of two evils for the occa-
sional traveler, but it became a "must" for those who required fast transportation. Trips were accomplished in
comfort more desirable than that offered by the backbreak-
ing road jeeps. Flying the 155-mile front which became
stabilized when the truce talks began took a matter of about
80 minutes by air. A trip by jeep took several days. Train
travel was slow and indirect. And with the establishment of
a stabilized front, more than 100 Army-built airstrips became available for the light planes which could transport
personnel quickly to within jeeping distance of any unit in
Korea.

It was in this setting that the first curtain of the act of aggression was raised at 0400 hours on 25 June 1950. Subsequently, the "cease fire and withdraw" dictum of the United
Nations Security Council was ignored on 26 June 1950. The
next day, United States Air Force and Naval units in the Far
East were ordered into the fray. As a result, military units
stationed in Japan were alerted for shipment to Korea. On
1 July, advance parties of the 24th Infantry Division arrived

in Korea and plans were made to establish Japan as the arsenal of the United Nations.

The only American troops in South Korea when hostilities broke out were the 500 members of the Korea Military Assistance Group (KMAG). This small group remained at its advisory posts within the ROK (Republic of Korea) Army units to guide the operations until help arrived. Among them were a few Army Aviators.

The outbreak of the war found the US 24th Infantry Division stationed in the southern Honshu-Kyushu area; the 25th Infantry Division was located in the south-central Honshu Area; and the 1st Cavalry Division occupied the Kanto Plain region in central Honshu. These were the three American combat divisions, fattened by almost five years of occupation duty in Japan and filled with green troops, which would attempt to stem the tide of North Korean aggression.

From this pitifully small beginning, hundreds of thousands of UN troops would subsequently see action in the struggle for Korea. Only a small fraction would be Army Aviators. But the exploits of these men, a handful at a time, spell their own vital role in a frustrating, vicious and bitter campaign. As the eyes of the Infantry and the lanyard of the Artillery, they fought their war in the air and won it on the ground.

An L-17 airplane, used to carry messages to division outposts, prepares to take off from the K-37 Airfield, EUSAK Headquarters, Taegu, Korea.
(U. S. Army Photo)

An L-4 plane lands after a mission, somewhere in Korea.
(U. S. Army Photo)

An L-5 used by Ground Forces in Korea to spot artillery being given
a pre-flight check. *(U. S. Army Photo)*

A small airplane belonging to the 3rd U. S. Infantry Division that was forced to use the bumpy Korean road for an emergency landing strip is towed to one side of the road to await the return of its pilot.
(U. S. Army Photo)

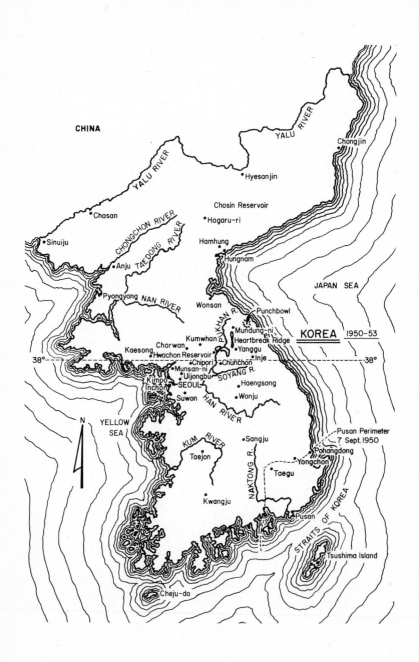

CHAPTER 2

THE PIONEERS

The record of Army Aviation operations during the early days is confused. But the confusion of the record merely reflects the military operations in a difficult terrain and the spontaneous conditions under which the military forces, totally unprepared for combat, were thrown into the line. The 24th Division aviation section was alerted for movement to Korea on 29 June 1950. Gas tanks were stripped from jeeps and installed in the rear seats of their L-4's for the flight across the Sea of Japan. This preparation brought back memories to the old-time Cub pilots who had been among the hundreds flying the English Channel to Normandy in L-4's similarly equipped with auxiliary fuel tanks during World War II. History was repeating itself. The logic of this planning paid off for Captain James C. Goode of the 13th Field Artillery Battalion. On 5 July, Goode flew across the Sea only to find the Korean coast closed in by weather. Because he had the auxiliary fuel tank in his L-4, Goode was able to return to Brady Field, Japan.

At approximately 2300 hours on 30 June, the 21st Infantry Regiment, stationed in Kumamoto, was ordered to proceed to Itazuki Air Force Base on the Island of Kyushu for movement by air to Pusan, Korea. On the morning of 1 July, Lt. Leonard T. Bolton and Lt. Richard H. Nelson departed in two L-17's from Brady Field, Japan, for duty with KMAG. The next day, these officers returned to Brady Field from Taejon. They were replaced by Lt. Robert Lessard and Lt. Thad L. Ferris, who reported to Maj. Gen. John H. Church, commanding general of the advance command of all American Forces in Korea. Lieutenant Ferris flew back to Japan on 3 July to lead the first contingent of L-5's to go to Korea across the Straits of Korea. His L-17 was used as the lead plane so as to have control of the flight and to maintain contact with the Air Force. The three L-5's in this flight were piloted by Lt. John Stanton, who was later killed in a mid-air collision with an F-51, Lt. George Rogers and Lt. James E. Alvator. These aircraft landed on the concrete airstrip west of Pusan. On 4 July, Lt. George Rogers

and Lt. James E. Alvator proceeded to the Taejon airfield
and then farther north to a fighter airstrip at Pyongtaek,
approximately twenty miles south of the Suwon airbase.
There the leading elements of the 21st Infantry Regiment and
its supporting artillery were contacted. The same day, nine
pilots of the 24th Division flew from Brady Field to Taejon.

Credit for the first Army Aviation mission flown in the combat zone is difficult to assess, since the record is confused
on this score. Sharing the honors on 4 July must of necessity be Lt. Alvator, Lt. Robert C. Adams and Lt. George
C. Rogers, all of the 24th Division aviation section.

On the afternoon of 4 July, at approximately 1600 hours,
Lt. Alvator was flying a mission in direct support of the
21st Regiment which at that time was of single battalion
strength. While adjusting mortar and 105 mm fire in support of the infantry, Lt. Alvator was jumped by three enemy
Yak-9's in the vicinity of Osan. Alvator managed to elude
the enemy aircraft, which proceeded to the Pyongtaek air
strip and strafed three light aircraft parked there. The
strafed craft were those of Lt. Wilford Giley, Captain Alexander Bolding and Lt. Robert Adams.

The Army Aviators conducted their operations during the
first days in Korea without benefit of assistance from their
ground crews. On 9 July, these crewmen reached Taejon,
the forward base of all light aircraft in Korea, after being
transported to the peninsula by LST from Japan.

The principal mission of Army Aviation during this period
was reconnaissance. Lack of any other means of communications placed a great responsibility upon the Army flyers
to provide the ground commanders with intelligence information which was badly needed. Because of the shortage of
troops on the ground, it became necessary for Army air
reconnaissance to spot the enemy forces so that the UN
troops already in the theater could be maneuvered into the
most effective defensive positions. It was a case of using
what troops were available in positions where they could do
the most good. Because of the rugged terrain features of
the battle ground, air observation was essential to accomplish the delaying action which was demanded by events.

When the 24th Inf. Div. was committed to battle, nothing
more than 2.36 rockets were available to stop the Russian-
built tanks with which the invading Red forces were equipped.
These tanks were so well camouflaged that UN fighter pilots
had difficulty finding them. Some enemy tanks which were

detected were found to be so close to the defenders' front
lines that the fighters hesitated to bring them under fire.

It was under these conditions that Army Aviation became
operational with VHF-equipped L-17's. With this radio
equipment, Army Aviators were dispatched on reconnaissance missions to spot the enemy tanks and to call in air
strikes upon them by the high-performance aircraft of the
Air Force. The L-17 was the only aircraft used at the time
by the Army in Korea which was so equipped that radio
communications with Air Force aircraft could be maintained.
And an effective means of communications was vital to the
successful use of ground support aircraft during those early
days when the only effective weapons available were those
of the Air Force. But because the L-17 was a low-wing,
multi-passenger plane designed principally for the transportation of personnel and limited cargo, it was not particularly suited for directing air strikes. Visibility was
limited for both pilot and observer, and maneuvering at
low altitudes to pick up obscure targets was hazardous. But
it was a case, again, of making maximum use of available
equipment.

Both jet and tractor types of UN combat aircraft were operating from airfields in the southern part of Japan to fly
their missions in direct support of the ground troops. During the first few days of hostilities, these airmen had little
difficulty in their operations because it was logical for them
to assume that any activity in the target area was that of the
enemy and therefore legal game for their guns. When the
24th Inf. Div. took the field, however, a problem of co-or-
dination presented itself.

Jet fighters from Japan were limited on the amount of time
they could safely spend in the target area before they had
to begin their long flights back across the Sea of Japan. It
was difficult for them to search, select and hit targets with
their limited fuel supplies. Another difficulty became
increasingly serious as more and more UN troops were
thrown into the fight. The fast-flying airmen could not dif-
ferentiate between friend and foe in the increasingly fluid
battle conditions. Many times the whole tactical situation
had changed between the time the flyers had been briefed
on their missions in Japan and their arrival over the target
area. The only obvious solution was to establish a system
of airborne control which could be used to direct them to a
target, brief them right over the combat area, and to make
visual adjustments of their strikes. But in order to put this
system into play, there had to be available the personnel

who were familiar with the current tactical operations on the ground, and they had to be equipped with the means of transmitting this information to the visiting jets. As a result, Army officers thoroughly briefed by G-3 were placed in the L-17's and sent on their way.

"Operation Dragonfly" was initiated on 6 July. Across the Straits of Korea and the Sea of Japan, fighter pilots taking off from their bases in Japan were instructed to fly to a designated area and to contact the controller who would be flying in a small aircraft over the front lines. For the first time, the airwaves of Korea were introduced to "Dragonfly", the radio call sign of the 24th Inf. Div. aviation section whose responsibility it became to usher the Air Force flyers to their front row seats in the war. The first mission was coordinated by Lt. Leonard T. Bolton and Lt. Robert N. Tedd who guided six B-26's and four F-51's to the destruction of a column of ten enemy T-34 tanks standing bumper to bumper on a road near Pyongtaek. The L-17 pilots guided the Air Force B-26's in a wing-tip to wing-tip attack on the tanks. The immediate effect was dirt and smoke over the target area. Low ceilings and smoke obscured the target so that the observers were prevented from gauging accurate results of the mission. The F-51's strafed enemy troops in the trucks to the rear of the column of tanks. Casualties to enemy troops and equipment were estimated at 75 per cent.

During the first week of July, leading elements of the North Korean armies had penetrated south of the ROK capitol of Seoul to a point about ten miles south of Suwon on the main Seoul-Taegu artery. Seoul had fallen to the Reds on 28 June, three days after the invading forces had crossed the 38th Parallel in nine different places. First contact with the invaders was made by elements of the 24th Division south of Suwon. The Army Aviation operations against the enemy were simultaneous with ground actions in the vicinity of Osan. Air strikes were directed to targets only 150 yards from the front lines where fighters were zeroed in on enemy tank columns which were destroyed with napalm. The L-17's from which control had been established were flown in lazy patterns parallel to the front lines not only so that maximum observation could be achieved, but so that they could act as markers for the bomb line which the attacking fighters needed to guard against dropping their bombs on friendly troops.

It was during this period that the North Korean soldier received his baptism of observation. Never before had he seen the small unarmed aircraft soaring lazily over his head. His immediate reaction was one of confusion. The planes did not fire on him, nor did they seem in any way aggressive. Past experiences with aircraft dictated that he take cover. Yet, when he did not, no danger was apparent. But it was not long before accurately adjusted mortar and artillery fire began to fall around him. He got the point quickly, that in some strange Western way the occupants of the little plane above him were firing the guns he could not see.

Immediately upon their arrival in Korea, the Army Aviators assumed a schedule of dawn-to-dark aerial observation. Their aircraft, which were war-weary before the Korean campaign, were now nursed into the air for mission after mission. Long supply lines had resulted in shortages of such luxuries as aviation fuel. Truck gas again served as a substitute, just as it did during the critical weeks following D-Day in Normandy during World War II. Spare parts for the aircraft were non-existent. All repairs were improvised. But in spite of these obstacles, the Army planes continued their low and slow flights over the battle zones, directing accurate and devastating fire on the enemy. The Taro Leaf pilots of the 24th Division flew at altitudes ranging from 500 feet to 2,500 feet above the terrain as they sought out enemy positions. The mission assigned to the Division was a delaying action to slow down the North Korean armies until other UN Divisions could be equipped and shipped to Korea.

Within a few days of its entry into battle, the Army Aviators of the 24th Division recorded their first casualty. Late in the afternoon of 7 July, Lt. Arvid O. Munson took off on a mission from the airstrip at Taejon. He did not return. It was not until Chonan was retaken in October that his body and airplane were found. It was believed that Munson had been shot down by machinegun fire behind enemy lines.

On 9 July, Lt. George Rogers wrecked the first aircraft through non-combat action when he hit a pole in the road on which he was landing. The aircraft somersaulted and burned.

As the 24th Division withdrew slowly down the Seoul-Taegu corridor, a heavy toll was taken of the personnel and equipment of the attacking forces. The 21st Infantry had been augmented by the 34th Regiment on 6 July. And in Japan, meanwhile, the 25th Inf. Div. was being readied for its role in the Korea campaign. Also, the 1st Cav. Div. was being brought up to full strength for movement by water to the peninsula. All the supplies stored in the depots throughout Japan at this time were being collected for shipment to Korea and for issue to units staging in the combat area. On 10 July, the Eighth Army aviation section arrived to begin its operations from Taegu. The 25th Division aviation sec-took off on its over-water flight the same day in World War II L-4's, L-5's and L-17's. The Cubs were equipped with auxiliary fuel tanks for the crossing. The Division did not arrive until 11 July, so that the aviation section had no ground crews, no gasoline and no equipment during their first day in Korea. The section moved up to Taegu on 12 July to begin its combat operations. On 17 July, the aviation section of the 1st Cav. Div. joined the battle.

The reactions of the Japanese to the departure of the occupation forces for the combat zone at this time surprised many a GI. Captain Philip Payne of Kansas, a veteran of four years of service in the Far East, later said that, "When the Korean deal broke out and the 1st Cavalry was on its way to embark for the fighting front, the Japs lined their route of march in tearful throngs. A lot of people who had come to know individual soldiers went to the temples to pray for their safety. Many a GI went to battle carrying a Japanese prayer bag which had been blessed in the temple. I still have the bag our housegirl gave me before I left. I carried it all through Korea, and I'm still carrying it in my right breast pocket. I'm not superstitious, but I feel better with it on me. It's just a little bag about four inches long and three inches wide. Embroidered in the silk is a prayer for the safety of the man carrying it. All Japanese soldiers carried one into battle during World War II. The point is, that the Japs took these GI's into their hearts while they were occupying their country. They tell me that never before in history have a conquered people prayed for the safety of their conquerors in battle. I don't know how true this is, but it certainly made an impression on me."

Many Army Aviators were later to have similar experiences as they passed through Japan on their routes to Korea. Since shoulder holsters for their pistols were not an item of issue by the Army, many of them paused during their short stays at Camp Drake to go to a little shop in the village of Okawa to purchase them. Just outside the gate to the camp and three doors east of the Busy Bee Gift Shoppe was a little leather goods shopkeeper who spoke fluent English. Without asking, he seemed to know when his customers were making their last purchases before joining the forces in Korea. After the ceremony of exchanging money was completed, he would wish the Army Aviator good fortune very sincerely and clasp his hands and say: "We all pray God for your safe and swift return."

Meanwhile, back in the Pentagon, Lt. Col. Claude L. Shepard of the Career Management Division, an old-time Army Aviator then in charge of the assignment of flying personnel, was wrestling with the problem of making available more Army Aviators to the theater of operations. Almost immediately, the recall of Reserve and National Guard flyers was ordered. Shortages of pilots in the Far East command were made up by a shuffling of personnel from rear area assignments. Those flyers who were already on active duty with the Army were to provide a stop-gap until enough recalled Reservists and newly-trained pilots could be sent to Korea. Top priority was given them for air transportation overseas. Plans were also made to expand the entering pilot-trainee classes from 100 per year to 100 per month, an increase of 1,200 per cent.

With the arrival of increasing numbers of Army aircraft in the Korean Theater, the task of plotting the movements and dispositions of enemy forces became less difficult. Division commanders were relying heavily on information received from the Army Aviators who were flying the front from morning until night. Because of the rugged terrain and the lack of Engineering equipment, their airstrips were small and rough. From the outset, Division commanders had requested that the aviation sections operate from fields as close to their command posts as possible. Commanders who had previously plotted their tactics from their CP's and had observed the war from Jeeps began to use the Army aircraft almost exclusively for orientation, planning and operation. Because of the congested and hazardous road conditions, field commanders also used the light planes as expeditious means of supervising the activities of their troops in zones of action. The communications difficulties during this period would have been insurmountable were it not for the light planes. The greatest percentage of information on the front line activities was supplied by the Army Aviators and more than 75 per cent of the artillery missions were fired by air observers. In addition, surveillance missions were flown over a vest area to detect any possible beach landings or flanking movements by the enemy. And the pilots averaged 100 flying hours a month for the first three months of the war. Lt. James Lawrence of the 8th FA Bn. logged 140 hours one month during that trying summer.

After the enemy's initial surprise at the appearance of the Grasshoppers, the Army pilots found themselves the targets of ground fire. The increased aggressiveness of the enemy against them left undeterred the Army Aviators who continued to fly their missions at low altitudes, just as they did during World War II. Their missions were now extended behind the enemy lines. And by probing into the enemy's backyard secrets, they were able to lend greater aid to the hard-pressed UN ground troops.

This change in tactics proved costly. On 14 July, Lt. Woodrow W. Brown of the 24th Division had three feet of his left wing shot off by enemy ground fire. With his observer, Lt. Sneller, Brown was able to glide back to friendly lines near Kongju for a landing only 50 yeard behind the UN outposts.

During this period, the Army Aviators became convinced that they would not be immune to enemy air attack. On 12 July, in the vicinity of Kongju, an L-4 manned by Captain Alexander P. Bolding and Lt. Robert C. Adams of the 24th Division was jumped by a pair of Yak-9's. The two flyers were covering the withdrawal of the 21st and 34th Infantry Regiments across the Kum River. While adjusting the supporting artillery of the 19th Infantry Regiment, the aircraft was hit. Adams, who was at the controls, began evasive maneuvers at low altitude with his stricken aircraft. As a result of his skillful flying, one of the Yaks in the slow-speed dogfight lost control and crashed into a hill. This was said by Army Aviators to be the first and only aircraft lost by the enemy which can be credited to an Army Aviator in the Korea campaign. Adams' L-4 subsequently crashed on the withdrawal route. Both pilots were seriously injured when they were picked up by the last medical evacuation litter jeep to leave the area. Lt. Adams was later returned to combat duty, but Captain Bolding was evacuated to the States for treatment of his wounds.

Just south of the same area on 19 July, Lt. John Dusell of the 24th Division was shot down by Yak-9's just north of Taejon. His observer, Lt. Bazzero, crawled from the wrecked L-4 and forced a Korean civilian to carry him on his back to Taejon, where he sent out a patrol to bring his pilot back.

"Operation Dragonfly" continued until November 1950. But on 14 July, the Air Force determined to try its hand at fighter-bomber direction from light planes. Air Force pilots and L-5's appeared in Korea to be indoctrinated by the 24th Division aviation section in the conduct of such missions. Their operation was dubbed "Mosquito" and the Air Force pilots used observers supplied by the Army. The L-5 "Mosquito" would later be supplanted by the T-6.

Although the fighting front had been in a state of continuous flux for the ground troops during this period, the aviation sections in action had established their bases of operation in static positions. The Army Aviators' missions during this period were being flown from the Taejon air strip. When the landing field came under mortar fire on 18 July, the 24th Division's aviation section was forced to make its first withdrawal to the south. This was the first of seventeen moves to be made in the next ten months. The enemy firing on the Taejon air strip resulted in the first casualty to be recorded among the ground crewmen. Corporal Herbert Fenner received shrapnel wounds from the mortar fire.

With the withdrawal from Taejon, the aviation section of the 24th Division was split. The L-17's were sent to the airstrip in Taegu. Two L-5's, one L-4 and two mechanics went to the east coast airstrip at Pohang with Lts. Rogers, Alvator and Melvin Perry. This aviation section joined with the 52nd F. A. Bn. in supporting the 21st Infantry Regiment which had been deployed to the east coast.

After the fall of Taejon, the rapid withdrawal of the UN troops forced aviation sections to take advantage of existing landing areas. No support could be expected from Engineer construction units which were swamped with higher priority missions.

The Kumchon airstrip is an example of the difficulties which this situation developed. Due to the absence of hard-surface areas along the withdrawal routes, a portion of the MSR in the center of the city was marked off as an aircraft landing area. Vehicular traffic was routed along a bypass road. The airstrip was short, barely long enough for takeoffs and landings under the best conditions. Obstructions at both ends of the runway increased the normal flying hazards. On one occasion, a pilot flying the assistant commander of the 24th Division was unable to gain enough altitude to clear obstacles on takeoff. As he rolled down the strip at increasing speed, the native huts came closer and closer, but he was still on the ground. He reached flying speed during the last third of his takeoff run, however, and was able to pull his aircraft up into a staggering flight path. When the pilot saw that he was not going to reach the margin of altitude he needed to clear the huts, he dropped the wheels of his aircraft onto the nearest thatched roof and bounced himself into the air for the additional inches he needed to clear his flight.

He made it.

At Pohang during the end of July, both Lts. Perry and Rogers were injured and evacuated for medical treatment, leaving Lt. Alvator as the only pilot for the three aircraft in his section. Because no replacement pilots were immediately available, the services of Corporal Cooler as a pilot were enlisted. Cooler held a private pilot's license and had been a mechanic with the section. Alvator checked him out in an L-4 and oriented him on the battle situation. Cooler began flying combat missions with the aid of an Artillery observer furnished by the 52nd F.A. Bn. The enlisted pilot's missions were alternated with those of Alvator for a period of five days.

Meanwhile, during the middle of July, Lt. James Hancock of the 25th Inf. Div. was credited with being the first Army Aviator to adjust naval gunfire in Korea. Using an L-17 which carried a ROK officer and an American Intelligence officer as observers, Hancock flew for nine hours on the first day of adjusting the fire of two US destroyers off the east coast. Their targets included enemy trucks, personnel and a communications station.

The 24th Division pulled out of the line near the end of July for a well-earned rest. They were relieved by the 1st Cav. Div. to the west and by the 2nd Division at Pohang. After three days near Taegu, the aviation section moved to Masan where they established their airstrip on the dock area and made their takeoffs and landings between warehouses.

CHAPTER 3

U.S.ARMY
14835

EBB TIDE

The Army Aviator's war was extended beyond the front line patrol stages during the first days of the 1950 campaigns. Hectic days darkened into uncertain nights as the weary pilots returned from flights of constant vigilance along the front, as well as behind the enemy's main lines

The enemy employed tactics new to the war during the first terrible month of fighting. Red troops infiltrated through the UN lines to cause great havoc. Dressed in the familiar white garb of the Korean civilian, these troops mingled with the refugees who were clogging the roads leading to the sanctuary of the southern peninsula. Once behind the fighting front, they discarded their civilian clothing and as newly-uniformed enemy soldiers they lay in ambush along the withdrawal route. The rugged Korean terrain afforded them many hidden paths and trails which they used to advantage for guerrilla operations in the rear areas. Therefore, Army Aviators took on a new mission of keeping up constant surveillance of "civilian" groups moving through the combat zones. They warned unsuspecting ground troops of impending ambushes. All MSR's were patrolled by Army aircraft. Suspected activities were noted and reported.

While the three American Divisions were establishing a line running generally west to east and north of Taegu, a new menace was discovered by pilots flying for G-2 and G-3 of Eighth Army Headquarters. These pilots had been given the mission of plotting enemy movements in the areas where elements of the ROK (Republic of Korea) Army were withdrawing. In the far western sector, a sizeable North Korean force had moved unchallenged down the coast and had begun to swing toward Pusan. Constant surveillance by Army aircraft bore out the fact that this was more than a diversionary movement. Information pieced together by G-2 showed that this strong force had as its mission the capture of the major port of Pusan which, if it fell into enemy hands, would deny the UN forces the logistical toehold they desperately needed to continue the campaign on the peninsula.

As a result of this important discovery by Army Aviators flying the surveillance missions in the area, a rapid shift of the 25th Inf. Div. from the Sangju area to the Masan-Chinju sector was immediately effected. Military experts who have since evaluated military tactics during the Pusan Perimeter operations feel that this one shifting of troops during the critical period had been responsible for the successful defense of Korea. But the silent partners still are the Army Aviators who had provided the military strategists with the basis for their effective planning.

The critical shortage of pilots during this period was such that Eighth Army aviation section drafted the services of Corporal A. C. Ewing, a former Air Force pilot serving as a mechanic with Eighth Army. Corporal Ewing flew 56 aerial reconnaissance missions during the months of July and August. His efforts played a major role in the plotting of enemy movements in areas outside the zones of the American Divisions.

The communications problem during the first month of the campaign was one of major importance. Reports from isolated areas could reach Eighth Army Headquarters only by word of mouth because of the severe shortage of signal equipment. As a result, the information was so dated as to be of little value to the military planners.

Lt. Gen. Walton H. Walker, Eighth Army commander at this time, realized the immediate value of Army aircraft. Every day he flew the front lines from one end to the other, visiting command posts, noting strong defensive positions, and generally doing his planning in the air. Upon his return to his headquarters each day, General Walker was able to provide first-hand information to his Intelligence officers who had no other way of getting the data. The situation was ironic. Here was the Army Commander briefing the officers whose normal duties required that they brief the Army Commander.

When the fall of Taegu appeared imminent, a small road behind the Eighth Army Headquarters was used as a pick-up strip for the Army Commander. The remainder of the headquarters established a command post in Pusan, but General Walker and his tactical staff remained in Taegu to direct combat operations. The first project handed to the Engineers at the new headquarters was the building of a light plane airstrip immediately behind the main CP. Thirty minutes from the time the Army Commander left his tactical CP in Taegu, he was in his office at the main CP. An aircraft and pilot were on constant alert to fly him to any combat area where dangerous changes in the tactical situation demanded his attention.

At the end of July, when the Naktong Perimeter had been established, the 24th Division had occupied an airstrip about 2,000 feet long and surrounded by obstacles. Aviators of the Twenty-fourth still speak with awe of the one incident they remember about the Miryang strip. It was a rainstormy night in mid-August when a quirk of the elements brought in to a safe landing an Air Force B-26 whose pilot was receiving landing instructions from Taegu radio tower and who landed 20 miles away at Miryang.

The UN forces were strengthened on 8 August when the 2nd Inf. Div., the "Second to None", which had been shipped direct to the combat zone from Fort Lewis, Washington, took its place on the fighting front alongside the battle-weary troops in the Perimeter. On 2 September, Captain W. L. Armstrong and Lt. W. A. Baugh flew the first 2nd Division air mission during the Naktong River operations. This action formed the prelude to the breaking out of the Pusan Perimeter by the UN forces. They flew an L-17 to lead Air Force fighters in close support of ground troops.

With four infantry divisions now on the line, the aviation communications problem increased greatly. VHF radios in the L-17's permitted the air controller to direct fighter strikes on only two channels. With five or six strikes being conducted at the same time, the effective use of these channels became increasingly difficult. Often, pilots had to repeat three and four times their instructions to the fighter aircraft. As a result, the element of surprise was completely lost. Many times jet aircraft were forced to abort their missions and to return to their bases in Japan before their fuel supplies became completely exhausted. Ammunition in such cases were expended on the homeward trip because of the danger of landing the aircraft with full loads of armed bombs.

In spite of these difficulties, however, Army Aviators were able to direct pin-point fighter missions in some instances as close as 25 yards to friendly positions. During these missions the light plane pilots flew as low as 50 feet to lead the fighter aircraft into their targets. From the first light of dawn to graying dusk, the airwaves of Korea echoed the call signs of the division air controllers: 24th Division's "Dragonfly", 25th Division's "Pickle Barrel", 1st Cavalry's "Pineapple", 2nd Division's "Horsefly", and Eighth Army's "Comet".

With the expansion of the tactical maneuvering on the ground, the role of Army Aviation gained in importance and expanded in versatility. On 28 July, the 27th Regiment of the 25th Division became the target of a major attack by the enemy in the vicinity of Hwanggan. During the action one company was completely cut off and isolated from the regiment. Aircraft from the Division aviation section were dispatched to drop medical supplies and ammunition to the hard-pressed company. With fresh supplies of ammunition, the company was able to fight its way back to friendly lines. The next day the aviation section repeated its resupply mission to elements of a company cut off from the 24th Regiment in the Sangju area.

Although supplies and a limited number of replacements were arriving daily, the tactical situation was becoming more precarious as the lines tightened around the cities of Taegu, Masan and Pohang-dong. Army spotters had little trouble finding targets for both the artillery crews and the fighter aircraft. Mission after mission was accomplished with excellent results. But the feeling persisted that the most vicious fighting was yet to come. When the UN forces could retreat no longer and they had to stand up and fight off the Reds without giving up any more of the precious ground, their backs would be to the sea and the only hope of salvation would be to attack.

On 29 July, General Walker issued an ultimatum to his troops, the gist of which was:

> "There will be no more retreating, withdrawal or adjustment of the lines, or any other term you may choose. There is no line behind us to which we can retreat. Every unit must counterattack to keep the enemy in confusion and off balance.
>
> "There will be no Dunkirk; there will be no Bataan.
>
> "A retreat to Pusan would be one of the greatest butcheries in history. We must fight to the end. Capture by these people is worse than death itself. We will fight as a team. If some of us must die, we will die fighting together. Any man who gives ground may be responsible for the death of thousands of his comrades..."

This was the Pusan Perimeter, the last desperate stand by the UN forces to retain their hold on the peninsula. The aggressor forces had driven the defenders into a "stand or die" position.

For the men of the 24th Division, the early days of the fighting had been bloody and humiliating, dirty and frustrating, and marked by death and heroism. They and the men who had joined them from Japan had fought through rain and mud, crawled through the stagnant, stinking waters of the rice paddies spiced with the earthy smells which even yet form his recollections of Korea. He was exasperated by the prickly heat of the incessant summer sun. The inescapable lice, fleas and mosquitoes irritated him. Bleeding, tattered, frequently hungry, he fought the enemy to his front, his flanks, and often to his rear. His enemy was the terrain, the weather and the Reds. They combined to stifle him in the enclosure that was the Pusan Perimeter.

As the war reached critical proportions, so did the battle of maintenance for the Army Aviation sections. Aircraft had to be pooled in order to fulfill more and more of the tactical missions demanded by field commanders. Army Aviators were no longer the lone sparrows of World War II who had worked independently with their parent units. It became evident to division aviation officers that individual unit aviation sections had to be combined into a single group so that maximum results could be achieved with a minimum of effort by the fast-deteriorating aircraft and the battle-worn personnel. The battalion aviation sections, jealously guarded as the individual properties of the unit commanders, were incorporated into division sections under headquarters control. The results were a saving of wear and tear on the already weary aircraft and pilots, a saving in the scarce supply of replacement parts and aircraft, and a greater efficiency in narrowing down the missions to a minimum of overlapping.

During the month of August, the UN forces were able to conduct limited offensives all along the front because of the arrival of replacements and increasing tonnage of supplies. As these attacks increased in frequency, the ever-present Army spotter plane was at the point of attack, dealing death and destruction to the enemy which massed like some gigantic horde of brown ants. It was during this period, too, that the first psychological warfare leaflets were dropped on the North Korean troops. Aircraft from Eighth Army flew up and down the line showering leaflets on the roads and strong points, urging the enemy soldiers to give up the fight.

As the battle line stabilized, guerrilla activities increased in the rear areas. On one occasion, a small enemy force succeeded in throwing hand grenades into two aircraft parked on the 2nd Division airstrip. Pilots in the aviation sections found themselves alerted constantly during the nights when guerrilla activity had been reported in the area. The light planes had gained a new respect among the enemy, who had placed them high on their priority lists for destruction.

General Matthew B. Ridgway boards an L-17 for a tour of the lines.
(U. S. Army Photo)

THE TIDE TURNS

To relieve the pressure against the defenders of the Perimeter to the southeast, the Tenth U. S. Army Corps embarked from Japan to perform an encircling amphibious landing at Inchon and to head south, north and east in the three-
pronged maneuver of "Operation 100-B". The landing was
made on 15 September to take advantage of the favorable
tides of the Yellow Sea. The "mystery corps" had been formed in secrecy and had landed its 300-ship invasion fleet after
record-breaking 30 days of preparation and in spite of a
typhoon which broke waves 30 feet high over the ships plow-
ing through the Yellow Sea.

The tide of battle changed abruptly with the landing of nearly
70,000 troops in the Seoul area. The X Corps had been made
up of the 7th Inf. Div., the 1st Marine Division and supporting units, including ROK's. The North Koreans had enjoyed
their greatest victories during the period 1 September to 11
September. On a coordinated attack in the eastern sector
and along the northern line, the enemy had advanced to within
seven miles of Taegu, had captured and lost Yongchon, had
penetrated the eastern zone to a point three miles from
Kyongju, and had taken the area of Pohang-dong where an
airfield vital to the UN effort was located. Excepting for
the thumbprint area of the Pusan Perimeter, the enemy had
conquered almost seven-eighths of the disputed peninsula.

But the tide had turned.

Meanwhile, in the western sector, aggressive action by the
25th and 2nd Divisions had prevented any major assault from
forming. During this period, despite low clouds and limited
visibility, Army aircraft continued their missions of combat
surveillance throughout the zones of combat. One occasion
found Major Walter Borden and Captain E. M. Lynch of
Eighth Army's "Eagle Flight" hit by enemy ground fire while
flying over Yongchon under a 300-foot ceiling. Such hazards
were taken in stride by the Army "flyboys".

For the first time during the Korean operations, light planes were used for reconnaissance deep into enemy territory, but not beyond the maxium range of friendly artillery. This was a far cry from the rule commonly accepted during World War II operations in Europe. There the Army pilots had flown the front lines at low altitudes in order that the light planes might elude any bandit aircraft crossing the lines.

Army Aviation was due its share of glory in the amphibious landings at Inchon. On 16 September, Captain Charles Keleman of X Corps made a takeoff in an Army L-5 from the carrier "Badoeng Straits" for a flight to Kimpo airfield a few miles northwest of Seoul. He was forced to return to the deck of the carrier, however, when he found that the airfield was still in enemy hands.

With the landing of X Corps at Inchon, troops in the Perimeter began a sustained attack on the North Korean armies that had confined them for two months of bitter fighting. With their Army planes buzzing overhead, the 2nd and 25th Divisions jumped off to the south on a coordinated attack with the 24th and 1st Cavalry Divisions to the north. By 20 September, all units were rolling through the rear areas of the enemy lines. The backbone of the NK forces was broken. Task forces, protected by an umbrella of friendly aircraft, moved over the network of roads leading to Seoul and a linkup with X Corps.

Enemy resistance was intense along the Seoul-Taegu corridor. The attacking 24th Division found the hills flanking the main road well defended by NK troops. Division pilots fired mission after artillery mission in an attempt to dislodge the die-hard defenders. On 18 September, First Lieutenant LaMonne, flying for the 6th Tank Battalion, was hit over the city of Kumchon. He was credited with being the first Army Aviator to parachute to safety during the Korea fighting. The next day, Lt. Richard Peterson was shot down by ground fire about 15 miles south of Kumchon. Meanwhile, the 1st Cav. Div. task forces were moving up the secondary roads to the north in an effort to cut off the enemy fleeing toward Seoul.

During their first two months in action, the 1st Cav. Div. aviation officer, Major James McCord, reported that his losses totalled six aircraft, one pilot and one observer killed, two pilots and two observers seriously injured.

From the 16th to the 20th of September, General Walker was in an Army plane constantly flying over the entire battleground to observe the results of the Eighth Army offensive. On 18 September, while the leading elements of the 24th Division were fighting for Kumchon, General Walker flew over the Taejon area in an L-5 to watch the North Koreans in their withdrawal to the north. This flight of 75 miles behind the enemy lines was the deepest of any flight in the Korean war by Army aircraft. Throughout the period, beginning with the break-out from the Pusan Perimeter until the link-up of UN forces in the vicinity of Suwon, General Walker had ventured deep into enemy-held territory so that he could gather first-hand information for his plan of cutting off the bulk of the North Korean army which was withering before the onslaught of his advancing Eighth Army.

Division aviation sections which had been operating off one field for so long a period of time during the stabilized fighting at the Perimeter suddenly found themselves moving rapidly from one hurriedly-cut airstrip to another. The tactical situation was fluid, but the flow was all in the direction of the enemy rear. Advancing units found their only means of communications to be the Army aircraft which were leading them on their advances. There was no time for intricate telephone nets to be laid.

The link-up of Eighth Army and X Corps was effected on 26 September, just south of Suwon near the west coast, when a unit of the 1st Cav. Div. met elements of the 7th Inf. Div.

Seoul was liberated for the first time by UN forces on 29 September. On 1 October, EUSAK announced that all organized resistance had ceased in South Korea.

Meanwhile, stateside developments augured well for the Army Aviation effort in Korea. The Army announced that it had ear-marked the expenditure of $42,376,230 for new airplanes during the fiscal year 1951. The original pre-Korea budget request had been only $2,000,000. Plans called for the purchase of about 500 Cessna L-19 aircraft to replace the obsolete aircraft then in use, and about 150 helicopters for both medical evacuation and troop movement missions.

With increased numbers of Reserve pilots being recalled for active duty, a 30-day refresher training course was begun at the Army Aviation School, Fort Sill, Oklahoma, in October, 1950. The course was to continue until March, 1952, when this category of pilots was exhausted. A total of 210 Army Aviators was graduated from this course. In meeting the demands for Army Aviators in Korea, the school also stepped up its training schedules so that by the end of the war, 1,484 pilots had been graduated with about 29 weeks of schooling.

Back in Korea, the UN forces resumed their pursuit of the enemy across the 38th Parallel near Kaesong on 19 October after a short period of regrouping. The North Korean capitol of Pyongyang fell to the Eighth Army the same day. The honor of being the first American soldier to enter the city was claimed by Sgt. M. V. Parker of the 2nd Division Military Police Company. During these operations, Army aircraft of the 2nd Division, operating off the Haeju airfield, scoured the hills for the fleeing enemy. The 1st Cav. Div., which was moving up the main road to Pyongyang, found their aircraft flying protective cover all along the route.

Army Aviators who were guiding fighter strikes from L-17's complained of "blind spots" they had found when looking out for other aircraft in their flying area. Any plane in front of them and at a lower altitude could not be seen, nor could any aircraft directly below or above them. In their missions of directing the strikes of high-performance aircraft, these pilots had found a need to divert their attentions from their missions to be doubly alert to avoid mid-air collisions. In spite of their precautions, however, some of these missions ended in disaster. One such fatality occurred on 18 October when Lt. John Stanton of the 24th Division aviation section, along with his observer, Lt. John Watkins, was leading four F-51's in a fighter strike in the vicinity of Sinmak. One of the fighters, in pulling up after a strafing run, collided with the Army L-17. All three of the flyers were killed.

The steam-rolling UN offensive ended at the Yalu. On 20 October, the 187th Airborne Regimental Combat Team parachuted near Anju, about 40 miles north of Pyongyang, in an attempt to rescue UN prisoners of war who, according to Intelligence reports, were being taken to the north by their Red captors. The airborne operation was also designed to cut off the Red armies fleeing to the safety of China. This operation was instrumental in permitting the forces in the western sector to move up rapidly to consolidate the line on the approach to the boundary of North Korea. The consolidation was accomplished generally along the Chongchon River. The 25th Division, meanwhile, had been retained in the Taejon area to round up straggler PW's and to neutralize the guerrilla activities along the MSR from Taegu to Seoul.

Increased enemy activity sprang up in the rear areas north and east of Kaesong. This was a hilly, thickly wooded area which afforded perfect terrain for a build-up of troops which could easily be hidden from ground observation posts. Army aircraft kept the area under constant surveillance. But the enemy had devised a new plan to neutralize the effectiveness of the spotting planes. By setting fire to scattered woodlands, the enemy was able to cut down visibility to a quarter of a mile in many areas. Under this clever smoke screen, they continued their build-up almost unmolested.

At this time, X Corps troops were diverted to the east coast offensive and were landed at Wonsan, which had fallen to I ROK Corps on 10 October. Republic of Korea troops reached the Yalu at Chosan on 26 October.

On 11 November, the Turks entered the Korea campaign. They were to prove themselves an excellent fighting force in the bitter battles to come. When the Turkish Brigade arrived in the Kaesong area to assist the 25th Division in its mission of clearing the rear areas of stragglers, their two L-18 Army aircraft (Piper Super Cubs) and two pilots took their places on the line with other UN light aircraft. These planes were the most modern to appear on the Army Aviation scene up to this time and for several months to come. Equipped with flaps and electric starters, they were an improved model of the sturdy L-4's of World War II.

While attempts were being made to neutralize guerrilla activities, disturbing reports were being evaluated at UN Intelligence centers. On 31 October, Intelligence revealed that 316, 000 Chinese troops were massed at the Manchurian border. In the eastern sector, contact had been reported with elements of the 124th Chinese Communist Division (CCF) on 1 November. Reports of the first ten days of November indicated the presence of at least 11 CCF divisions in the forward areas. Contact with these units by UN forces had been brief, but a constant build-up of this new enemy had been reported by aerial observers. A prisoner captured by the 2nd Division on 4 November reported that 50, 000 CCF troops had crossed the Yalu into Korea.

It was during this period that the Army Aviation sections met still another enemy with the coming of the cold weather. Poor planning for winter operations hit at the flyers almost as hard as it did the GI's in the foxholes. Because of a lack of adequate cold weather equipment and clothing, pilots flying their unheated aircraft could remain in the air for relatively short periods of time. Planes that had been war-weary at the start of the campaign had become almost unflyable. Every flight should have been their last. But the ingenuity and dogged determination of the ground crews who suffered most from working unprotected in sub-zero weather kept the planes in the air for day after freezing day of that first terrible winter. Forced landings resulted from mechanical difficulties. One division counted seven in a single day. Replacement engines arriving from the States were found to have been improperly overhauled, and more headaches resulted.

By 20 November, the U. S. 7th Inf. Div. had reached the Yalu at Hyesanjin. These were the first American troops to reach the Chinese frontier. On 24 November, the Eighth Army jumped off all along the front to bring about a showdown with the CCF troops which had been playing a cat-and-mouse game with the UN forces approaching the Yalu. The showdown was not long in coming, and the UN victories proved to be short-lived. In the bitter cold of that North Korean November, the Chinese "Volunteers" joined with the remnants of the NK armies in a counter-offensive which stretched all along the Eighth Army front. General Douglas Mac-Arthur's much publicized expectation that he would have his troops home by Christmas was shattered. A heavy engagement was met in the vicinity of Tokchon. The 2nd Division felt the full fury of the Chinese attack early in the morning of 26 November at Kune-ri. In below-zero temperatures, the "Second to None" fought off wave after wave of fanatical Reds who were sweeping into their positions.

A general withdrawal of UN troops began. It was a retreat which rolled with the punch of an estimated 200,000 of the new enemy for almost 200 miles to the south.

During this enemy offensive which was to be recorded for all time as one of the major battles of the century, Lt. Robert A. Michelson of Long Beach, California, assigned to the 5th Light Aviation Section (LAS) of X Corps, was flying ammunition and medical supplies in his L-5. Return trips were made carrying wounded from the front lines to hospitals in the rear areas. During one of his trips from Sagaru-ri, which was surrounded by the enemy, Michelson was forced to circle the icy airstrip while bulldozers manned by UN Engineers cleared it of the Red dead. The pilot was able to evacuate 27 critically wounded UN soldiers and Marines to Hamhung during the period.

It was not until October of the next year that the 7th Inf. Div. aviation section was rewarded for its role in the historic November offensive. This section became the first in Army Aviation history to be awarded the Distinguished Unit Citation. This honor was conferred upon the "Hour Glass" Division flyers for their evacuation of wounded during the Chosin Reservoir operations in November, 1950. During a week-long operation, using every plane they could get into the air, the pilots of the Seventh evacuated more than 800 critically wounded soldiers from the enemy trap and flew them to Hamhung, 60 miles away. On their trips to the pick-up site, they brought vitally needed medical supplies, food and ammunition to the troops struggling to hold the line.

On the western flank, elements of the 21st Regiment of the 24th Division were but ten miles south of the city of Sinuiju when they were forced to withdraw to the Chongchon River at Anju. With this withdrawal began the long trek back to the defensive positions below the 38th Parallel. Elements of the 2nd Division moving southward out of Kunu-ri toward Sunchon were ambushed. All personnel able to make the march had to leave their vehicles and attempt to return to friendly lines on foot. Again Army Aviators came to the assistance of ground troops. Equipped with maps, pilots who could be spared from the aviation sections of the 24th Division, Eighth Army Headquarters and other units flew over the area looking for stragglers. Upon spotting a group, the pilots marked their position on a map, drew an arrow to point the avenue of escape, and dropped the map to the surprised troops. Air sections of all the divisions were expending maximum efforts at this time in an attempt to help neutralize the effectiveness of the Chinese attack. The 1st Cav. Div. was protecting the right flank of the besieged 2nd Division until it could withdraw and regroup. The 25th Division moved in support of the units pulling back from the northern defenses. After the initial confusion, the withdrawal became orderly and the UN troops moved to new defensive positions with a limited number of casualties. The bitter cold was taking its toll, however, and the evacuation of sick and wounded was slow and difficult.

By 11 December, the Marines and the 7th Division had broken out of the Chosin Reservoir encirclement. The November offensive had cost the Americans the loss of 12,000 killed, wounded and missing, plus huge amounts of equipment.

The Navy came to the assistance of the ground troops in the northeast sector during this time. And teamed up with the floating artillery of the battleship USS Missouri were the aviators of the 3rd Division who adjusted fire even at night in the vicinity of Hamhung.

The first main line of defense for the west sector was established south of the Imjin River where a delaying action was planned to allow the evacuation of all the equipment and supplies which were stored in the Ascom City area just west of Seoul. The rapid withdrawal of the UN forces allowed them a breathing spell from the Chinese onslaught. Defensive positions were strengthened for the fresh fighting which was sure to come.

But there was no breather for Army Aviation. As a result of their surveillance missions which plotted the movements of the enemy, probing attacks began along the new line on 23 December. This was the day on which General Walker, the Eighth Army commander, was killed in a jeep accident while on an inspection trip to the 24th Division headquarters. His death was particularly tragic at a time when his forceful leadership was sorely needed for the crucial days which lay ahead. And by his death, Army Aviation had suffered the loss of one of its most enthusiastic supporters.

By Christmas Eve, X Corps had evacuated the east coast from Songjin to Hungnam of 105,000 troops, 17,600 vehicles, 350,000 tons of equipment and 100,000 refugees. The "Dunkirk" which had been feared by Americans at home had been averted in 12 days of feverish activity. The next day, the Chinese Communist forces crossed the 38th Parallel at Haeju on the west coast of the peninsula. A general drive to the south found Seoul exchanging hands for the third time when NK-CCF troops recaptured the city at about 1400 hours on 4 January 1951.

Meanwhile, on 27 December, Lt. Gen. Matthew B. Ridgway had assumed command of the UN forces under the control of Eighth Army. He was to become a familiar sight at airstrips throughout Korea in the jump boots and hand grenades strapped to his shoulder harness which earned him the code name of "Grenade Six".

During the winter of 1950, another Army Aviation "first" was recorded when Captain Marcus L. Sullivan of Big Sandy, Texas, became the first Army pilot to fly an Army helicopter (Bell H-13 B) in Korea at Ascom City.

During this same winter of 1950, Lt. Clifford B. King of

Raleigh, Tennessee, was awarded the Distinguished Flying Cross when he broke up a threatened attack by a force of 1,000 Chinese soldiers marching down a road approaching the left flank of the newly-committed 3rd Inf. Div. King was on patrol behind enemy lines when he spotted the Red forces. He called for artillery, but none was in position to bring effective fire on the target. King spotted an Air Force "Mosquito" plane in the area and was able to point out the target by flying low over the enemy who took him under heavy ground fire. The lack of VHF radio equipment forced King to these extreme measures. But the expedient worked and an air strike was finally brought in to break up the threat. In a later action, King received the Silver Star for chalking up 1,300 Red casualties in the "Valley of Death", a 1,000-yard long valley near the 38th Parallel. Among the targets destroyed were pack animals and supplies. King made three trips in marginal weather by flying at 300 feet among jagged peaks until his mission was accomplished.

By this time Army Aviators in Korea had been impressed with the viciousness of their three enemies: the weather, the terrain and the Reds. The World War II postage stamp landing areas which had been loudly bruited by freshman proponents of Army Aviation did not exist in Korea. Engineer-built airstrips became a "must" to their operations. Korean weather timetables were as vicious and unpredictable as the Red enemy. And the Reds swatted at the light, unarmed and unarmored aircraft as they would at annoying horseflies.

The maintenance problem, meanwhile, was being given some attention by the "powers" who were relying on Army Aviation with almost childlike faith during the trying campaigns. According to Army Aviation School records, the availability of mechanics was ample during the first stages of Korea because of the shortage of aircraft. But as more aircraft became available, the supply of mechanics was extremely short. In the theater of operations, therefore, many auto mechanics were trained to work on the aircraft. At the beginning of the Korea operations, an Ordnance Light Aviation Maintenance Company (OLAM) of the 79th Ordnance Battalion had been split up in Japan and shipped to the fighting front in Taegu. The complete organization was transferred to Korea in October, 1950. During the following months, two OLAM companies, the 71st Ordnance Depot and the battalion headquarters were set up for full operation, with their base located at Ascom City. These units assumed the responsibility for providing parts and aircraft as they became available in short supply from the States. They also supported field units with shop repair facilities. But their job was one of a frustrated skirmishing with inefficient supply channels.

On 1 January 1951, the Chinese unleashed the full fury of their attack on Eighth Army. Again Army Aviators played a vital role in the success of the withdrawal which resulted. With accurate adjustment of artillery fire and fighter missions against the pursuing Chinese and North Koreans, the Army flyers gave the ground forces sufficient time to pull back to prepared defenses with a minimum of casualties among UN troops and a maximum of losses to the enemy.

Seoul fell to the Communists on 4 January, but the foresight which had resulted in the evacuation of all UN troops, supplies and equipment left the enemy with a hollow victory. After the successful evacuation of Hungnam and Hamhung, the 7th, 1st Marine and 3rd Divisions joined forces below the 38th Parallel. The 7th and Marine Divisions occupied the eastern sector, while the 3rd Division was shifted to the far western flank.

The board was set for a new ride on the Korean teeter-totter.

CHAPTER 5

BEGINNING
OF THE END

The new year in Korea found Army Aviators flying compassionate missions as well as those of tactical urgency.
In January, 1951, Captain Albert C. Sebourn of Fort Smith,
Arkansas, flew the first Army battlefield evacuation mission
in a helicopter. This mission was accomplished in the Seoul
area.

Although Captain Sebourn's 2nd Army Helicopter Detachment
had been in operation less than a month with their Bell H-13's,
its four pilots achieved such a record that they were awarded
the Distinguished-Flying Cross on 14 January. With four
helicopters, Captain Sebourn and his pilots evacuated 23
badly wounded soldiers of a battalion completely surrounded
by the Reds. They flew their patients to a hospital 25 miles
to the rear in a period of two and a half hours. On their
return trips, the helicopters carried rations and 10,000
rounds of ammunition. These supplies sustained the surrounded battalion until reinforcements helped to drive back
the enemy. The helicopter mission of 14 January proved
to be their baptism of fire. One of the H-13's suffered ten
direct hits by enemy machine gun fire, but none was serious
enough to interrupt its operations.

The 2nd Army Helicopter Detachment, using only its four
helicopters, brought out more than 500 wounded in the period
of January 1 to February 1.

The first fatality connected with Army helicopter flying was
reported on 24 February. The aircraft carrying Maj. Gen.
Bryant E. Moore, commander of the IX Corps, struck a
power line near the Han River east of Seoul. Neither occupant
was apparently injured by the crash, but General Moore died
shortly after when he suffered a heart attack. He had been
in the Far East only a month when he died. Reports of his
death have laid the cause to the helicopter accident, but the
Army record is clear that General Moore died of a heart
attack a short time later. The first fatality resulting directly from a helicopter crash was not to occur until almost
two years later.

The introduction of the helicopter as an Army vehicle in a combat theater proved a boon to the ground commanders who could make speedy inspections of even the most inaccessible combat positions. And for some of these commanders, the helicopter became the object of more personal consideration. Lt. John Hodges, son of Major General Hodges, deputy commander of Eighth Army, was critically wounded in April and was evacuated by helicopter. His flight in the H-13 was credited with saving his life, since the nature of his wound would not have allowed him to survive a trip by vehicle over the rough roads.

This was only the beginning of the amazing record of service which the helicopter was to compile during the Korean war. Without helicopter evacuation, hundreds of United Nations troops would have died of wounds before they could be treated effectively. But with the speedy and useful helicopters, prompt medical attention was made possible and the fatality rate for wounded soldiers was cut to less than half the World War II rate.

During the Civil War, 14 of every 100 wounded soldiers died. This figure was cut to eight in World War I. In Korea, only two or every 100 wounded died as a result of military action. So rapid was medical attention to become in Korea, and so excellent, that Assistant Secretary of Defense Melvin A. Casberg has said:

> "If I had a choice of being shot down and critically injured on 16th Street in Washington, D. C., or in the main line of resistance in Korea, I would have chosen the main line in Korea. Such professional care we have never had before. We have had top-notch men on patient evacuation with helicopters."

The first two weeks of the new year found the 2nd Division in a fierce battle against overwhelming odds. The enemy, attempting a major thrust from Hongchon to the vital road center at Wonju, ran head-on into advancing elements of the "Second to None". The battle raged back through Hoengsong, into Wonju, and back up the high ground just south of this strategic city. General Ridgway had ruled that Wonju must be held at all costs. He recognized that whoever controlled the five-pronged road hub controlled central Korea. Wonju served as an important rail terminal on the Kyonggang railroad leading to Pusan. The city also marked the center of the Eighth Army front.

The Communists' winter offensive was stopped cold in the Wonju-Chipyong-ni area, with the 2nd Division later pushing north of Wonju to Hoengsong. Enemy losses were heavy. The UN forces again took the initiative when enemy pressure diminished later in the month along a general line where UN forces had first engaged the enemy more than six months before. Targets for Army Aviators were lucrative. And the CCF offensive was stopped two months and 200 miles after it had begun far to the north.

By 11 February, the left flank of the UN line extended just south of the capital city of Seoul. But in the central sector, in the vicinity of Hoengsong and Chipyong-ni, another enemy build-up was reported by the Army pilots.

Orders to abandon Hoengsong were received during the early night hours of 11 February. The Netherlands Battalion and a company of the 7th Inf. Div. were fighting a delaying action to the south. To the west, meanwhile, troops of the 2nd Division girded themselves for the impending enemy assault. The next day was comparatively quiet, but Army air spotters reported the southward movement toward Chipyong-ni of large masses of enemy troops.

Brig. Gen. George C. Stewart, assistant commander of the 2nd Division, arrived in Wonju late in the evening of 12 February to assume command of the defense of the city. He called a meeting of all local unit commanders. There was to be no withdrawal and no evacuation of men or supplies. Everyone would stay, he said. A perimeter defense was to be organized so that massed fires could be placed on every approach to the city. Air observation pilots were ordered to fly their missions throughout the daylight hours to warn of approaching enemy troops or of impending attacks.

Historians of the 2nd Division described the subsequent action:

> "As daylight broke on 15 February, the Army Aviators of the Second had their planes in the air to seek out the enemy. First reports told of two Chinese divisions moving in a column southward along the Som River with the obvious intention of encircling the defenders of Wonju. They could see elements of the enemy column peeling off toward Wonju as it marched southward. Every available artillery piece in the Second Division and supporting Corps artillery was laid upon the marching mass of men. Thunderous barrages

roared across the hills as tons of shrapnel poured into the plodding troops. Thousands of shells wrought havoc never before seen on any army as the pilots reported the river running red with the blood of the massacred troops. Still they came, heedless of the carnage around them as they crawled forward. Hour after hour the unbelieveable carnage mounted as dog-tired, exhausted artillerymen slammed an endless stream of shells into the exposed masses of Chinese who continued to press forward. The staggering losses began to tell. The once-full enemy ranks were now thin, blasted, shocked remnants without leaders, without hope. Slowly, as though dazed, the remains of the ranks broke. Now only unorganized bands of useless bodies, they tried to escape north out of reach of the murderous guns. The cracking rain of steel followed them northward and air (power) took up where artillery could not reach. The attack was broken, the threat to Wonju was no longer critical."

The fierce battle had raged until 16 February. During this period, the aviation section of the 2nd Division alone was credited with 5,000 enemy casualties in the Wonju sector.

Eastward, the "Hour Glass" and 1st Marine Divisions maintained a steady advance which kept the enemy off balance and prevented them from organizing for an effective counterattack.

The tactical situation during the Spring was fluid. As a result, infiltrations by both sides were common. Army Aviation sections were not immune to ground actions, as was indicated by a report of the 24th Division aviation section which told of being overrun by the point of two enemy divisions near Hyon-ni. The enemy attacked during the early morning hours of 24 April, but they were beaten off by friendly quad-fifty fire. No casualties were reported, but one aircraft was completely destroyed, another was hit but salvaged, and a jeep was destroyed.

With the approach of Spring, Army Aviators were heartened by the arrival of a new all-metal, higher-powered observation plane to replace their out-dated, war-weary aircraft. On 16 February, the first Cessna L-19's were delivered to front line units. The L-19 "Bird Dog" experienced its baptism of fire in the ground actions which resulted in the second liberation of Seoul by UN forces on 18 March 1951. The arrival of the new aircraft brought a new era of compara-

ON 16 FEBRUARY 1951, *the Army aviators were heartened by the arrival of a new aircraft, the all-metal L-19 "Bird Dog" which was to receive its baptism of fire in the battle for the second liberation of Seoul.*
(Photo Courtesy of Cessna)

tive comfort to the Army Aviator. The beaten and battered L-4 and L-5 aircraft were replaced as rapidly as the L-19's arrived. The change brought a new fighting spirit to the pilots who had nursed their fabric-covered war horses through the long days of bitter fighting. The L-19 was a high-wing, tandem-seating, 213 horsepower aircraft equipped with a built-in VHF multi-channel radio, flaps, heater, electrical system and primary blind flight group of instruments. For the old-time Grasshoppers, stepping into the L-19 for the first time was like driving a Cadillac after months on a farm tractor.

With the coming of the L-19, too, a new safety device was introduced to the Army flyers. The new aircraft were equipped with shoulder harness which served to hold flyers fast in their seats in the event of a crash landing. During World War II, many serious injuries could have been averted had the Cubs been equipped with the harness. Before the Korean war was to end, many a flyer would have occasion to thank the Army for having provided the safety device and to thank his own good sense for making use of it.

The bravery of the Army pilots had been put to the test time after time during the comparatively short history of Army Aviation operations. The Army had taken official notice of the heroic deeds of individual Army Aviators on many occasions. The Navy presented its highest award for valor to an Army Aviator on 5 February 1952, for a rescue operation on 20 February 1951 by Captain John Olihovik of the 7th Inf. Div. who landed his L-16 in a creek bed behind enemy lines to rescue a Navy pilot from his wrecked Corsair fighter. The citation read:

> "... When a Navy aircraft was hit by enemy ground fire and crashed into the river bed of the Chu'chon-gang, Captain Olihovik, flying an unarmed plane, proceeded immediately to the area and, skillfully landing in the rough terrain, made his way on foot to the stricken aircraft despite intense and direct fire from enemy troops only 300 yards away. Reaching and lifting the critically injured pilot, he carried him back to the rescue plane which was idling 100 yards distant. Miraculously escaping almost certain death, injury or capture, he took off and flew the injured man directly to the Chech'on airstrip where he was quickly transferred to a field hospital. By his daring initiative and superb courage, he served to inspire other pilots to heroic efforts, thus contributing to the effectiveness of the striking power in the task force as a whole. His selfless devotion to duty in the face of grave personal risk reflects the highest credit upon Captain Olihovik and the United States Armed Forces..."

Although the Spring of 1951 was a period of limited offensives, General Ridgway spent an average of two and a half hours a day in the air. His whole day's planning was centered around air transportation from division zone to division zone. His pilots flew him in all kinds of weather, regardless of ceiling or visibility, so that the decisions which he alone could make were immediately available to his field commanders.

The aerial command post had come into its own because of the dictates of rugged terrain which demanded that the troop commanders see at first hand what their troops must do and how they were to do it. And there proved to be no more efficient method to accomplish this than by making full use of the small aircraft which were within a moment's reach.

The Ridgway plane was parked only a few hundred yards from his tactical command post. At his request, all regimental headquarters were easily accessible by Army aircraft. His daily visits to the frontline troops served as a great morale factor, since his presence proved an inspiration to the combat troops under his command. His frequent and unexpected visits to the fighting front would have been impractical were it not for the light planes which could be landed in the scores of small airstrips scattered throughout the peninsula.

One example of his intense interest in the fighting men of the Eighth Army was shown during "Operation Tomahawk" on 23 March. In order to cut off the enemy forces withdrawing from Seoul and vicinity, the 187th RCT was dropped 24 miles behind enemy lines at Munsan-ni. General Ridgway, in an unarmed observation plane, flew to the drop zone to watch the landing of the first elements of the regiment. He was landed on a small road in the drop zone soon after the first two elements had jumped. From the ground he watched the arrival and drop of the third group. Ridgway remained in the perimeter to conduct the operation personally. The General, it will be remembered, had served as a parachutist during World War II.

Army Aviation operations expanded with the arrival of new equipment. On 13 April, Major Robert L. Hoffman of the 2nd Division and his observer, Lt. Lee R. Hartell, expanded the night flying missions which had been conducted with much less formality heretofore. Hartell was killed in August, 1951, and later was awarded the Congressional Medal of Honor for bravery in continuing to direct artillery fire after his forward observation post was overrun. The target area for the night flight was the south edge of the Hwachon Reservoir. Major Hoffman reported his flight in detail:

> "The 2nd Division airstrip was lighted by using cans of sand soaked with gasoline used as flare pots to outline the limits of the usable runway. This method of lighting airstrips had been used quite successfully many times in the past. One new method used in lighting, however, was the positioning near the runway (within 50 yards) of a standard searchlight capable of turning a 360-degree radius, plus the capability of throwing a vertical beam for homing.

> "Take-off time was 2300 hours and was accomplished without difficulty. After climbing straight out to an altitude that would clear the hills in the vicinity of the airstrip, we circled back and established communications with the section base set (SCR 608) which had been moved up beside the searchlight for the duration of the mission.

"Communication was established and maintained with this base set without difficulty. The flares on the strip were checked for spacing and the searchlight was played on the surrounding hills and pointed skyward so that the pilot and observer could get an idea of how these facilities appeared from altitude. All this was done before the aircraft proceeded to the target area. We followed the MSR to the target area in order to stay completely oriented. With the light of the half-moon that shone throughout the mission, no contact with the horizon was lost. The prominent river and reservoir in the target area were sufficiently discernible to insure orientation. Lights on supply vehicles were valuable in following the MSR, since the road could not be seen. The L-19 aircraft was used on this mission and the panel lighting arrangement proved highly satisfactory.

"Position lights were left on during the mission except when actually observing artillery firing and locating the target area. It was found that the white lights on the top and bottom of the fuselage are quite blinding. The bulbs of these two lights should be removed before a night mission is attempted. After arriving in the target area, the searchlights directed at the target itself were readily observed. After establishing communication with the Division Artillery S-3, the searchlights were adjusted more exactly from the air and it was found that to facilitate this adjustment, a suitable radio should be set up at the searchlight sites. In the target area, the highest mountain was nearly 6,000 feet high. In order to avoid this obstruction, altitude of the aircraft was maintained at 7,000 feet. It is believed that if the terrain had not been so rugged as to require this extreme altitude, the mission would have been more easily accomplished.

"The target picked for this mission was on the south edge of the reservoir. After locating the proper spot (a boat landing site) we notified the fire direction center that we were in position to observe. The volleys fired were picked up easily and an adjustment was made. Subsequent volleys were observed, but no further action could be seen or taken from the air. Had the target been anywhere but on the edge of the Reservoir, it is extremely doubtful that it could have been located from the air. The moon's reflection on the water helped greatly in locating the target. The searchlights were a tremendous aid in keeping oriented, but the light thrown on the target was negligible as far as air observation was concerned. Ground observers could possibly benefit from the light, but looking down from above gives the impression of a white line on a blackboard. One very distracting element discovered during the mission consisted of the hundreds of grass, shrub and wood fires burning over the entire front. The reflections in the plane's plexiglass hampered our observation and the fires made pin-pointing anything on the ground practically impossible.

"After finishing our adjustment on the initial target, we were asked to observe a TOT (time on target) on the crest of the highest hill in the area. The searchlights were laid in the direction of the target, but the location of the lights in a defilade resulted only in diffused light on the hill. The TOT was observed and the effect reported as to pattern and firing. No adjustment was possible since the exact target could not be pin-pointed, even by using a brush or wood fire burning in the area. After observing and reporting the TOT, we were instructed to return to base. At this time, the base radio set was contacted and the request was made for the vertical homing beam to be displayed. The beam was readily picked up at a distance of nearly 15 miles. We flew directly to the beam without regard for position over the ground.

"The let-down was made by spiraling directly over the field and around the vertical beam. After reaching an altitude where surrounding hills could have been a hazard, the beam was directed at the extreme peaks and rotated in front of the circling aircraft. After lining up on the runway, the beam was placed parallel to the strip and at a slight inclining angle to serve as a guide for a possible go-around. An uneventful landing was made on the first pass at the field. The flight had lasted two hours. "

Major Hoffman completed his report with recommendations for pilots attempting similar flights in the future:

"Night missions should be performed only under the most ideal conditions, i.e., direct moonlight, aid of searchlights, pilot and observer completely familiar with the target area through extensive daylight flights and orientation, accurate maps, suitable airstrips, perfect communications and aircraft. Departure from these standards should be made only in emergencies. Parachutes should be currently packed, extra flashlights should be available in the event of failure of the plane's electrical system, chutes and shoulder harness should be worn as well as safety belts. Carburetor heat should receive special attention at night. Even though capabilities are greatly reduced during night flights, after-dark missions could prove valuable in emergencies. Care should be taken to use a minimum of aircraft in any single area because of the dangers of collision. If it is necessary for more than one aircraft to be operational, takeoff times, landing times, altitudes and radio channels should be staggered. Missions of this type, if accomplished in any volume, would be detrimental to the normal daylight operation of missions expected at division levels."

One of the most spectacular defense stands of the war was made by the 2nd Division in what later was to be known as the "May Massacre".

During the last days of April, Army air observers had reported the build-up of enemy troops and materiel. Air reconnaissance during this period was especially difficult because of a great pall of smoke which was hung out over the front by the enemy. Smoke pots burned day and night to mingle with the dust rising from the roads leading to the north.

The front was quiet in the eastern sector during early May after the Hwachon Reservoir activities found the Reds again heading northward. The ominous lull was pondered by Eighth Army Intelligence officers. Captured prisoners confirmed the suspicion that the Reds were preparing for another drive southward. Then it was learned that the Red forces had halted their trek to the north and were swinging to the southeast. According to Intelligence information, Red political leaders were forecasting great new victories for the brown-clad soldiers jogging back to battle through the mountains. Warnings to conserve their newly-issued rations of dried corn, fried flour cakes, kaoliang and rice were spiced with stories of great fleets of planes and masses of tanks which would support the coming drive.

In promising a great victory soon to be realized, the commissars baited the enthusiasms of the common soldier with the proposed destruction of the 2nd Division, an enemy of

China since the Boxer Rebellion. To fall with the Second would be the flanking ROK units. And the route to the south would be open.

Each day, more evidence was gathered by Intelligence officers to support their suspicions that the Second was to bear the brunt of an enemy offensive. But the Division G-2 could not believe the reports of the numbers of the enemy gathering for the attack when these reports streamed in from Army Aviators during the day of 14 May. The alert airmen late that afternoon reported thousands of enemy troops moving along a trail between Naepyong-ni and Sapkyo-ri toward the Division's positions.

Up to this time, a rationing of artillery ammunition had been in effect. The caution of the Division Intelligence personnel in allowing the expenditure of rounds in answer to the desperate pleas for fire missions from the Army air observers was apparently dictated by this condition. However, when ground observers substantiated the air reports of large enemy troop movements, Batteries of the 503rd, 196th and 38th FA Battalions were ordered to adjust their fire on the rapidly approaching Communists. It was almost too late.

The frustration of the Army Aviators who had been sending appeal after radio appeal for artillery fire to deaf ears was boundless. But they became too busy executing their missions during the next days to remain bitter. During the eight days following, the Division requests for air observation could not be satisfied as pleas were continual for more planes to be made airborne.

Captain Bruce O. Ihlenfeldt of Lawton, Oklahoma, was serving as operations officer at the time. It was his unenviable responsibility to schedule extra missions for pilots and observers who had already put in long hours over the front. In his memory, the name of one observer stands out as being the most frequent volunteer: Lt. Lee R. Hartell of Danbury, Connecticut, 15th FA Battalion.

Hartell was a slightly-built five foot ten who had earned a reputation as a hustler with a great sense of humor. His fellow airmen remember him as "a real Artilleryman who could adjust the firing of several battalions of artillery simultaneously and play them like a piano".

During the Massacre, Hartell is remembered as the only observer who would be asking for "just one more" even after he had flown five missions in a single day. His record of time in the air during the eight days of the Massacre was 111:25 hours, an average of almost 14 hours a day. The record is unbelieveable, but it is certified in the log of the 2nd Division aviation section.

Hartell was later killed in action. (pilot fatigue)

During most of the May Massacre operation, the cloud ceilings were so low that normally the aircraft would have been grounded. But the situation was so critical that observation flights were made at 500 feet above the ground instead of at the usual three to four thousand feet. The fact that the Division lost not one plane under these hazardous conditions is nothing short of a miracle.

On 14 May, Army air had reported the enemy build-up of troop concentrations south of Yanggu and large movements along the south shore of the Hwachon Reservoir.

The May Massacre began at 0300 hours on 16 May with a preliminary attack by an enemy force against the 5th and 7th ROK Divisions on the 2nd Division right flank. Although the Chinese pressed their attack until dawn, they were forced to withdraw into the village of Hachon, which was then subjected to heavy UN artillery fire. By 0800 hours, the entire ROK sector was under heavy attack which forced all units to withdraw from their positions to a new line south of the Inje-Hongchon road. This withdrawal bared the entire east flank of the 2nd Division. The gap was filled by artillery concentrations fired on enemy groups encountered by 2nd Division patrols and as a result of air observation.

It was obvious to the commanders that the long-expected offensive had begun. Later Intelligence reports revealed the full extent of the assault. Four Chinese armies, consisting of 12 full-strength divisions of 175,000 men, had rolled into the 2nd Division zone. The mission of one Red army was to penetrate the ROK positions on the right, then to turn behind the Indianhead Division and envelop the right flank. A second army was to make a frontal assault, then split and move onto the flanks while a third army passed through as a column of divisions in thundering assault against whatever UN forces might be resisting the spearheading Red army forces. The fourth army of the assaulting forces would concentrate its efforts on the line north of Pungam-ni to the east.

The battle raged throughout the night of 17 May, with the Army Aviators of the Second awaiting daylight to resume their exhausting flights of the previous days. A maximum effort was called and pilots and observers flew mission after mission to keep the ground commanders informed of new concentrations of the enemy, as well as of the fast-shifting movements of troops as they weaved into battle. The assaults of wave after wave of fanatical Communists bent the UN lines and stretched them to critical tension. But they refused to break. They sprang back instead at the enemy with hastily organized provisional companies of headquarters and Engineer troops who left their pencils and bulldozers to fill the breach and keep the lines intact. Searchlights were used to illuminate the battlefield during the early morning of 17 May. Their beams helped the hard-pressed troops to locate and slaughter the onrushing Chinese.

When 17 May dawned, it found the battle still joined despite the staggering losses which the Chinese had been absorbing from rolling barrages of artillery fire. The French Battalion was committed to replace the 2nd Battalion of the 38th Regiment. By noon, the 23rd Inf. Regt. (less one battalion) was brought up from Division reserve to strengthen the line to the east. During the day, the ROK forces withdrew from their positions on the right flank, leaving a yawning gap to which the Chinese were pouring their reinforcements. Maj. Gen. Clark L. Ruffner, the Division Commander, called on the Dutch Battalion to close the gap opened by the retreat of the ROK's. His orders were to attack. Anxious to see at first hand the Dutch operation in this critical area, Ruffner summoned his Army helicopter to take him to the scene near Hill 1051 directly south of Sapkyo-ri. At about 1500 hours, the helicopter engine failed. The frail craft plunged to the earth and crashed on a rocky crag within sight of the enemy. Fortunately, both the General and his pilot escaped injury, excepting for bruises. The craft was completely demolished.

All limits on the expenditure of artillery shells had been lifted, meanwhile, on orders from General James A. Van Fleet. During the first 24 hours of the offensive, 30,000 rounds of artillery ammunition had been expended to stop the first gaps which had appeared in the line. General Van Fleet had assumed command of Eighth Army on 14 April when General Ridgway had been relieved to replace General Douglas MacArthur as Far East Commander. The limitations on ammunition expenditures had been in force because of the precarious tactical situation and the slow-arriving supplies from the States.

One of Van Fleet's first orders to Eighth Army commanders
had been that there would be no more withdrawals anywhere
along the front under any circumstances. When the Reds
were making their main attack on 17 May, the clouds were
down on the hilltops on either side of a valley through which
were pouring the brown-clad enemy troops by the tens of
thousands. Meeting them was a flight of four L-19 aircraft
flying low under the clouds to adjust all of the Division's
artillery. Adding to the confusion was the presence of Air
Force fighter aircraft which appeared in the valley each time
the ceiling lifted enough to allow them to grope their ways
through the draws leading into the valley. Often the air was
so packed with L-19's, F-51's and F-80's working over the
enemy forces that the pilot's chief concern was to avoid mid-
air collisions. The hazards of the air operations were increased because the artillery was using proximity fuses which
were set to explode the shells whenever they came within
short distances of solid objects.

Shortly after midnight on 19 May, fresh waves of Reds attacked along the modified "No-Name" line which ran in a north-
easterly-southwesterly direction just south of Hill 1051. The
line was so-called by General Van Fleet because in the confusion of drawing up the battle plans for the sector, staff
officers had neglected to label the line with an appropriate
code designation. The Red attacks took on suicidal proportions for a period of 90 minutes as five battalions of artillery
kept a stream of high-explosive shells in the air, cutting
down the attackers as they flung themselves against the bar-
bed wire, the mines and the rain of fire poured on them by
the men of the Second. In one eight-minute period, more
than 2,000 rounds of artillery were fired in front of one
company alone. Late in the afternoon, pressure of the enemy
attack was eased considerably all along the front. During the
last 24 hours, a reported 44,000 rounds of artillery fire were
delivered to the enemy. Although the enemy attacks along
this front continued through 22 May, their intensity was
meager in comparison with the bloody fighting of the first
days.

Daylight patrols now encountered little opposition so that
the time was ripe for a planned counterattack. At 0800 hours
on 23 May, the 2nd Division drove against the desperately
tired enemy who no longer had the numerical strength or
supplies to continue the pressure. This counterattack marked
one of the most dramatic achievements of the war. Their
pincers movement reached for Inje, a strategic location in a
deep valley surrounding the MSR and the Soyang River to the
northeast.

The May Massacre ended with the taking of Inje and the capture of the commanding peaks in the rugged hills forward of the village on 5 June. For the first six days of the Red offensive, the 2nd Division had fought a determined enemy, giving ground slowly while inflicting casualties estimated at 10,000 daily for each day. The term "May Massacre" resulted from this total of 60,000 enemy killed in the short period of time.

The role of Army Aviation during the entire period of the defensive action and the counterattack was closely connected with the ground action. Constant air activity of the aviation section of the Division was responsible for an estimated 60 per cent of the casualties among the enemy. Their continuous dawn-to-dusk flying missions proved them to be a worthy partner of the fighting team. And the May Massacre of 1951 proved to be the prelude to the Red bid for peace.

The Massacre will be long remembered especially by those on the spot who waited with baited breath the climax it would bring. On 11 February 1953, when General Van Fleet· was leaving the Far East for retirement in the States, newspapermen asked him what he considered to be the most significant landmark in Korea.

> "Well," he replied, "I could close my eyes and picture all of Korea, but the part that stands out and I remember most clearly is the mountainous area where the Communists tried to come through the 2nd Division in the Spring offensive of 1951. I can fly over that area and pick out knolls and little hills that even the smallest 2nd Division units were on.

The next month, June 1951, the anniversary of the Korean war found the UN troops in complete control of the tactical situation. Theirs had been a long and bitter campaign frought with the frustrations of green troops, confused tactics and the leaky supply lines which were overextended through 5,000 miles of ocean. For one of the few times in American military history, defeat - bitter and almost hopeless - had been tasted. American dead had been strewn on frozen mountain trails. The living had crawled forward in their tattered uniforms and broken shoes in the cold of that first terrible winter to seek out the enemy. And they were driven back in worse condition. They had climbed mountains and had waded streams to save themselves at Hungnam, while an anxious free world waited with prayers for this magnificent army which surely could not have escaped the Red trap. But they made it. And when they did, they aroused a new hope which found its beginning in June 1951.

And sharing this hope, just as they had shared the dangers, the privations and the death throughout the campaign, were the Army Aviators.

General Matthew B. Ridgway and Admiral C. Turner Joy meet at Munsan-ni where the "peace camp" was located as a headquarters for the UN negotiators at the peace talks. (U. S. Army Photo)

CHAPTER 6

PEACE TALK

When the UN troops crossed the 38th Parallel for the third time, they assaulted the enemy build-up area of the "Iron Triangle" (Chorwon - Pyonggang - Kumwha). This action took place on 24 May. A month later, on 23 June, the Soviet delegate to the UN, Jacob A. Malik, proposed a cease-fire in Korea.

The first year of the war ended. Army Aviation looked back on many "firsts" which had revolutionized the tactics developed during World War II. Now the light planes were used to guide high-powered fighter aircraft in direct support of ground troops. Almost every branch of the service used the light planes in missions ranging from carrying the mail to the evacuation of the wounded. The helicopter was introduced as a battlefield vehicle. And on 22 March was established the Eighth Army Flight Detachment (8085th Army Unit) which was known initially as the "Eagle Flight" and later as the "Dragon Flight". Its mission included the transportation of members of the Army staff sections throughout Korea. This was the first such unit ever to be activated during hostilities in an active combat theater. One of the Flight's early missions was to bring delegates to the cease-fire conferences which were held at Kaesong during the period 10 July to 2 August. These days were filled with charges and counter-charges of neutrality violations which caused delays and a final change of the conference site to Panmunjom.

The beginning of the truce talks filled an anxious world with an expectation which was doomed from the start, as later history proved. False rumors of a cease-fire agreement led soldiers on the front lines to adopt the attitude that they would not fire unless fired upon. This was interpreted by the Reds as a sign of weakness which should be exploited. And subsequent action on their part belied the eloquently-voiced desires for peace which had been echoed in June. In the Punchbowl area in the northeast sector that Fall, a Red offensive reflected the ulterior motives of the Communists in requesting the peace talks.

Captain Ashby Snow of Salt Lake City had been annoyed during this period by ground fire from enemy troops. With his observer, Lt. Bill Dobbs of Mineral Springs, Arkansas, he took his L-19 (number 1460) on a Red-hunting mission. Armed with a carbine, Dobbs sprayed the annoying enemy, who scattered in surprise.

The Army Aviators were discovering that talking peace could be more dangerous than fighting the war. On the west-central front, the Army flyers found an increasing flak activity against them. On 25 October, the 1st Cav. Div. lost a plane in flames. Only one of the flyers was able to parachute out of it.

The recollections of Captain Lloyd O. Borgen of Brooklyn, N. Y., point up the hazards of the period:

> "Lately, the flak has been getting pretty heavy. One outfit lost a plane from 20 millimeter flak, but the pilot and observer are still living. The shell came in through the bottom of the plane and blew the rear throttle quadrant all to hell in the observer's face and also blew out all the plexiglass except the windshield. The observer, naturally, was pretty badly cut in the face, whereas the pilot didn't get scratched. A few weeks ago, another outfit lost a plane and they still haven't heard any more of the pilot or observer. And it seems to be getting a little rougher. Especially when we remember that the oldtimers here used to fly down valleys and buzz Chinks... now we still fly from 5 to 10 miles behind the Chink lines, but we keep about a 5-6 thousand foot altitude.

> "However, with field glasses, which we use all the time, we can still pick up a lot of good targets. The Chinks still walk around in the open and maybe take pot shots at us. We fired on one artillery position recently and just after the third round landed 10 yards from the piece, the damn Chinks fired again. They must have either been deaf, or just didn't give a damn. It isn't too often that you catch them firing artillery. They're getting to be like the Krauts... only shoot when they feel pretty sure you can't see them..."

Many of the Army pilots at this time began to complain that they could no longer contact the Air Force planes for ground strikes. A common remark by the Army pilots was:

"I guess the Air Force got teed off or scared that the Army is trying to take over control and have changed their radio frequencies. "

One reliable source reported:

"Now we can only watch them (the Air Force fighters) strafe and bomb on barren spots with no effect, while we know that there are a hundred Chinks probably a hundred yards away. The Mosquito pilots are a crazy bunch, they have lots of guts. They fly their T-6's at a couple of hundred feet over the Chink's lines and up to 6-7 miles behind them. That's bad enough, but to avoid being shot to pieces, they keep weaving violently back and forth so we just can't see how the observer in the back seat of the T-6 can do any good, let alone trying to observe out of a T-6 in straight and level flight. We're fighting now to get the old set-up back in effect. The funny part is, most of the Mosquito pilots agree that the old way was best for them, too. But I guess the brass have other ideas on their desks. "

This was the prelude to the bloody fighting for Heartbreak Ridge. During this period, the 2nd Division had pioneered the mass resupplying of troops from light planes. A battalion was resupplied in a mass drop north of Yanggu from an altitude of 150 feet. On 18 September, the planes were loaded with pilot, "kicker" and eight cases of C-rations. Cooks, mechanics and medical aid men volunteered to kick out the rations.

One of the strangest therapies of military medicine was inadvertently applied by Lt. Gene Rughlander of the 8191st Helicopter Detachment on 7 September. The pilot had taken off in his helicopter with a soldier who had been wounded in the chest. A blood clot was forming at the base of his throat and threatened to cut off his breathing before he could reach a hospital for treatment. On the takeoff from the forward aid station, the helicopter struck wires and crashed. Rughlander was badly injured in the crash. But by some quirk of fate, the shock of the hard landing broke the blood clot in the wounded soldier's throat and saved his life.

In October, the battle of Heartbreak Ridge ended in victory for the UN forces.

"Heartbreak" was a narrow, rocky mountain mass running north and south in the northeast sector of the front above the

38th Parallel. Its three peaks dominated the Mundung-ni and Satae-ri valleys. The south and east slopes were extremely steep. From these slopes the "Punchbowl", which had already fallen to the UN forces, could be seen to the north. Heartbreak was important because in each valley bordering the ridge were two vital roads and stream beds. The roads were secondary class routes, but a road capable of moving military traffic was built in a short time. Also, a twisting, turning, boulder-strewn stream bed in each valley furnished an approach for tanks. Enemy bunkers guarded the key ridges. Due to a moderate slope to the west and north, the enemy's supplies could be moved up into their positions with a minimum of effort. And since the ridge provided an effective natural barrier to a straightening of the front lines to the west, its capture became of prime importance to UN troops marching northward.

The battle for Heartbreak began on 13 September when the 9th Inf. Regt. of the 2nd Division launched an attack on Hill 728, located to the south and west of the main objective, Hill 931, which was the central peak of the three heights on the ridgeline. The three peaks were Hill 894 to the south, Hill 931 in the center and Hill 851 to the north. Hill 894 was taken at 1445 hours on 15 September by the 9th Inf. Regt. after the unit had been diverted from its original objective to the west. This "Manchu" Regiment had secured the entire ridgeline to the south and west when a coordinated attack by the 23rd Regiment to take the remaining peaks in the ridgeline failed in spite of close air and artillery support. The enemy fought with fanatic determination to retain control of the vital ridge. Eighth Army lifted all limits on the expenditure of artillery ammunition as it offered every support to the 2nd Division in its attempt to take Heartbreak Ridge.

Before the bitter fighting had begun on the Ridge, heavy vegetation had covered its slopes. But air strikes and artillery destroyed all natural means for individual concealment. The air became thick with blue smoke from exploding artillery shells and the peaks were churned into pulverized rock. The Ridge took on the appearance of a forest after a fire. Only the twisted, charred remains of trees and shrubs remained as blackened evidence of greener slopes.

Shortly after midnight on 18 September, the 23rd Regiment reached the crest of Hill 851 to the north. But their victory was short-lived. With daylight, the holding company was wiped out after fighting hand-to-hand when their supplies of ammunition ran out. Two battalions of the regiment tried for Hill 931 on 22 September without success. But after four determined assaults on 23 and 24 September, the First Battalion grappled with the enemy and literally crawled its way to the top in spite of pelting mortar, grenade and bullet. Here they took their places among the dead in the Red-built bunkers. Until 0220 hours on 24 September, they were able to hold the position. One hour and ten minutes later, the thinned ranks of the battle-weary "A" Company were forced off the ridge by screaming North Koreans who charged in mass, throwing grenades and directing murderous fire into the bunkers which they themselves had built originally.

Another attempt at the capture of Hill 728 to the west by the Manchu Regiment had been repulsed the same day. The need for regrouping, resupplying and preparing the units for new assaults on Heartbreak caused a lull for two days. During this time, poor visibility hindered all attempts at positive action. On 26 September, the French Battalion tried its luck against Hill 931, to no avail. In spite of repeated attempts during the rest of the month to dislodge the enemy from the Ridge, the end of September found it still in enemy hands, although they had been decimated by the loss of 20,000 casualties.

The first day of the new month brought with it a new plan to uproot the enemy. A concentrated attack up both valleys by tank-infantry teams spearheading the advance of three regiments became Operation Order 37 for Heartbreak. The target date for "Operation Touchdown", as it was labelled, was to be 5 October at 2100 hours. By 1800 hours that day, every available truck which had been pressed into service had stockpiled more than 45,000 rounds of artillery ammunition, 10,000 rations and 20,000 gallons of gasoline. The supply dumps were stocked in a valley near the MSR to the west which was easily accessible to the entire field of battle.

In the overture to the battle, raiding thrusts by tanks were conducted every day from 3 October until the jumping-off two days later. On 4 October, the 2nd Division aviation section (code name "Ivanhoe") increased the tempo of its operations by firing on targets during the daylight hours against the enemy's harassing mortar and artillery fire.

On the night of 5 October, "Operation Touchdown" moved out with all the regiments on the line. The 2nd Battalion of the 23rd Inf. Regt. moved from its position on the southernmost of the three ridges (Hill 894) and after a brief but sharp firefight, took the commanding peak of Hill 931 by 0300 hours of 6 October. By 0630 hours, the hill was secured after a tie-in had been effected with the French Battalion to the west in the Mundung-ni Valley. To the southwest, the 38th Inf. Regt. took Hill 728 with little trouble and tied in with elements of the 23rd Regiment on the ridgeline west of Hill 894. Meanwhile, the tank-infantry task forces moving up the valleys on both sides of the Ridge were fighting to secure the high ground against counter-attack. By 10 October, this was accomplished and the task forces were sent northward to Mundung-ni and Satae-ri to close off the area. On 12 October, Hill 851 was attacked by the 23rd Regiment. After an all-night battle against North Koreans who threw arcs of fire down the slopes and who lobbed hand grenades into the faces of the attackers, the Regiment won its month-long battle for the ridge at 0630 hours.

Reconnaissance of Heartbreak Ridge by Army aircraft after its capture revealed why it had been so hard to take. According to historians of the Second:

> "Hill 931 itself was the center peak of three that were within small arms range of each other. While continuing to hold it, the enemy could put down well-aimed and observed fire in the neighboring two peaks. But what added even more to its strength for the North Korean defenders was the fact that its slope on the eastern side facing the 2nd Division troops was rocky and almost perpendicular for the last 200 to 300 yards. Ascent by foot troops was necessarily slow. On the reverse, or western side, the slope was less steep and was of dirt. Into this slope the enemy had dug his many bunkers of such strength as to resist even a direct hit from our 105 mm howitzers. These bunkers, about 25 yards from the topographical crest of the hill, were numerous enough to provide complete protection to some 400 to 500 men. During artillery or air bombardments, the enemy troops would leave their entrenchments and communications trenches on the crest for the protection of their strong bunkers. Yet, when the artillery or air attacks were lifted, they had ample time to return to their positions before our troops could scale the last very steep and rocky 200 to 300 yards on the attacking side. "

It was during this campaign that another "first" was established by Army Aviation. Captain George B. Daniels of Charleston, S. C., dropped flame throwers to hard-pressed infantrymen who were stalled in their attack on enemy-held bunkers. The two weapons parachuted to the ground were in action within two minutes. A third flame thrower was needed, so Lt. Ed Zeigler of Philadelphia loaded the weapon into his helicopter and landed almost on top of a surprised infantryman in a foxhole about 100 yards beyond the point where Daniels had dropped the first two weapons.

> "Just what in hell are you doing here?", asked the amazed GI.

Zeigler silently unloaded the weapon he had been carrying in one of the litters.

> "Here's the weapon you asked for."

Zeigler then took off before the infantryman could thank him.

Daniels was awarded the DFC for his part in the flame thrower drop. The citation accompanying the award read:

> "Captain Daniels was advised that an infantry unit, engaged in an attack against a fanatically-defended, enemy-held hill (near Mundung-ni) was desperately in need of flame throwers to dislodge the hostile troops from their elaborate fortifications.

FOR HIS HEROIC ACHIEVEMENT *in supplying the flame throwers to the infantrymen on Heartbreak Ridge, Capt. George B. Daniels was awarded the Distinguished-Flying Cross. Lt. Col. J. Elmore Swenson, EUSAK aviation officer, made the presentation.* (U. S. Army Photo)

"Realizing the risk involved, he immediately loaded one of the necessary weapons aboard a light, unarmed aircraft (L-19) and flew to the scene of the fighting. Flying low over the battle area, well within range of enemy fire, Captain Daniels made repeated passes over the terrain to find a suitable drop zone. After dropping the flame thrower, he returned to his base, loaded another weapon, flew over the same hazardous route and dropped it by parachute to the hard-pressed infantrymen.

"The heroic achievement of Captain Daniels enabled the friendly troops to dislodge the foe and to capture a hill of vital strategic importance with a minimum of casualties."

In a subsequent action, Daniels won the Silver Star when he laid telephone wire to infantry units under fire. He was accompanied on this 27 October mission by Captain Robert H. Bennett of Little Silver, N. J., a Signal Corps officer.

Heartbreak Ridge had produced a spectacle of fighting by all Army units which will forever stand out in military history.

A wire-laying dispenser improvised by the 2nd Division Signal Company was used in the Fall of 1951. The container holds four canvas WD-1 dispensers held together with old pieces of metal culvert and bolts and attached to wing shackle on the L-19. (U. S. Army Photo)

But the historical significance to the United Nations was even greater because the fighting produced evidence that China's entry into the war as an active partner had resulted from the almost complete destruction of the North Korean army as a fighting force. Heretofore, the CCF participation in the fighting had been limited to action on the western half of the front. On 16 October, a patrol from "G" Company of the 23rd Regiment had captured a prisoner who was identified as a member of the 204th CCF Division. The picture was completed by Intelligence officers who now determined that the 2nd Division was fighting CCF forces on its left flank and North Koreans on its right. The evidence of this relief of NK forces by the CCF was eloquent proof of the staggering losses which had been suffered by the NK forces in the operations along Heartbreak and Bloody Ridges.

The truce talks, which had been suspended during the Fall of 1951, were resumed at Panmunjom on 25 October. With the delegates to the talks based at Munsan-ni, Army Aviation was called upon to play its part in the negotiations by transporting mail, liaison personnel and distinguished visitors to the "peace camp".

One of the most precious cargoes carried by light Army aircraft throughout the campaign was blood plasma. Given top priority during transportation from the States, the plasma was flown to Korea through an easy 7,000 miles compared to the last few miles it had to travel to be of any real value.

Captain Robert R. Harding of San Antonio, Texas, participated in a plasma delivery flight under extremely hazardous conditions on the night of 10 October. Harding assigned himself the flight when, as operations officer of the 2nd Division aviation section, a call from the Division surgeon had requested him to seek a volunteer to fly blood into an unlighted, unused forward airstrip surrounded by hills 1,500 feet high.

At about 2200 hours, Harding and his crew chief, Corporal Laurence F. Anderson of Los Angeles, took off in an L-19. Anderson had volunteered to accompany the pilot and to hold six bottles of the precious fluid to keep them from jarring during the flight. Within a few minutes they had located the forward airstrip which was located in a deep canyon. At the first pass into the field, Harding missed the strip entirely, so he applied power and circled for a second attempt. Spurred by the clattering of his engine, medics of the 3rd Clearing Platoon at the airstrip ran a jeep to one end of the runway and played its lights to mark the landing area. Two cans of gasoline were lighted to indicate the far end of the strip. Captain Harding at this time was guiding his airplane from his daylight recollections of the strip's layout, since it was now completely dark. He made a safe landing on the second try. But Corporal Anderson said later that he would always remember the short twelve inches by which they missed a ridge line in making their last pass at the field. As a result of the flight, made under extremely hazardous and unusual conditions, the lives of several critically wounded soldiers of the 9th and 38th Inf. Regt. were saved.

In his recommendation that Captain Harding be awarded the Silver Star for this mission, Lt. Col. Lloyd R. Stropes, the division surgeon, wrote:

> "During the day of 10 October 1951, the patient load was extremely heavy. During the evening, the number of seriously wounded rose alarmingly and so depleted the supply of blood. The material could not be re-supplied by vehicle because the rough roads would cause it to hemolize. In a desperate attempt to get this critical material to the clearing platoon, the airstrip was called and asked that the trip be made. Captain Harding volunteered to go. (In so doing) Captain Harding risked his life by attempting an extremely hazardous mission."

Harding was awarded a Bronze Oak Leaf Cluster to his already-won Air Medal. Corporal Anderson received the Air Medal.

During the Winter of 1951, the combat lines were pretty well stabilized. The variety of missions undertaken by Army Aviators continued. Artillery combat missions were maintained on their dawn-to-dark schedules, special infantry missions were flown, combat commanders spent more and more time in Army aircraft to visit the front lines, and evacuations of wounded reflected the ground actions. By the end of the year, the Department of the Army had reported a total of 1,600 pilots on duty, including nearly 200 in Korea. Numbers of aircraft in use totalled 1,570. Of these, 380 were located in Korea. The year-end statistics released by Eighth Army were revealing.

1. During the period 4 July 1950 to 31 December 1951, Eighth Army light planes had totalled 140,792 missions during 186,372 hours of flying.

2. The unarmed planes flew 64, 541 combat missions.

3. Emphasis was placed on the fact that 90 per cent of the UN's deadly accurate artillery fire had been adjusted by the light planes.

4. Casualties during the 18-month period were listed as nine pilots and three observers killed in action; ten pilots and eight observers wounded in action. Only ten planes were lost in action, while non-combat accidents reached the total of 122.

On 3 November, Lt. Robert A. Michelson of Long Beach, California, and his co-pilot, Lt. Col. Joseph D. O'Hanlon of Los Angeles, evacuated by L-17 a Marine who had been wounded in the eyes. The flight was made at night and the Marine, Corporal John A. Vogel of Randolph, Massachusetts, made it to a rear area hospital in time to save his sight. The return flight by the Army Aviators was made the same night.

During the Heartbreak Ridge operations, Major Robert L. Boatright of Santa Monica, California, the aviation officer of the 2nd Division, was credited by grinning infantrymen with killing two North Korean soldiers when he accidentally dropped a C-ration box behind the enemy lines. The rations were intended for the UN infantrymen dug in on the crest of a hill. But Boatright overshot his target and the heavy carton ricocheted into the enemy soldiers standing close together over the hill watching the air drop. This contact with the enemy should have entitled the Californian's L-19 to wear the insignia showing two sickles crossed with forks. But Boatright was not aware of his contribution to the war effort until later.

Major Boatright added to his distinctive career the experience of receiving the first honorary membership in the 231st French Battalion to be awarded to an Army Aviator. The recognition resulted from Boatright's activities with the French Battalion, which had been attached to the 2nd Division during the Yanggu operations. The emblem of membership consisted of a diamond-shaped badge showing a mailed fist carrying a sword which crossed a gold olive branch at its tip. Inlaid between was a Tricolor bearing the letters "ONU" (Organization des Nations Unis). Upon receiving the insigne, the name of Boatright was added to the list of 2, 249 persons so honored. But the name of this officer is the first after which appears the designation "Army Aviator".

The extent to which Army Aviation by this time had become

established as a vital partner in Army operations in Korea was best expressed, probably, by Colonel William A. Mc-Caffrey of Newport, R. I. The commander of the 31st Inf. Regt. told newsmen that the small planes had become as much a part of the Army as the canteen and rifle.

One of the few parachute jumps by an Army Aviator during the combat operations was made on 28 December by Lt. Melvin K. Goulding of Austin, Texas. His L-19 was hit through a wing tank by enemy fire near Hill 1290 in the north-east sector during a routine observation mission. The plane caught fire. With his observer, Lt. Chester A. Huff of Hunt-ington Park, California, Goulding parachuted to safety. Both airmen were rescued by friendly troops near the front lines and were treated for extensive burns about the face and hands. Goulding was returned to flying duty after several weeks of hospitalization in Tokyo. On 7 May 1952, he was enrolled as a member of the Caterpillar Club, that exclusive organ-ization of flyers who had saved their lives by parachuting from an aircraft.

When Goulding returned to Korea ten weeks later, he was able to recount his own "clank" story. At noon on that fateful day, the two 7th Division Artillery airmen were flying at 7,000 feet to adjust fire on enemy mortar positions near the Punchbowl, about three miles behind enemy lines. Flying his twenty-sixth mission in three weeks on the front, Goulding was putting his aircraft through evasive maneuvers as he circled the target. Because of the high wind, he varied his altitude at each upwind turn since he found that his aircraft was being held almost stationary as it came into the wind. As Goulding guided his L-19 in a turn directly over Hill 1290, he felt a slight shuddering when the plane was hit by a single 20 millimeter shell which passed through the left wing's gas-oline tank. Fire broke out immediately under the leading edge of the wing. Goulding instinctively turned the stricken aircraft southward toward friendly lines. As the whole left side of the aircraft (number 14692) became engulfed with blazing fuel, the pilot attempted to blow the flames away from the cockpit by slipping the plane to the right. The ma-neuver was unsuccessful. Goulding reached for the radio microphone hanging to his left in order to air his predica-ment. But he pulled his hand back rapidly when it was burned by the hot instrument. At 6,000 feet he levelled off. The cockpit was filled with choking fumes. He turned to his ob-server and shouted for him to jump. Then, Goulding slid his seat forward and pulled the door's emergency release handle to his right. By the time the door had fallen off, Huff was in position to jump.

> "But he hesitated so long I was wondering what could be holding him up," Goulding said later. "I found out afterwards that Huff had been burned so severely that his right hand couldn't grasp the D-ring of his chute. He had to pick up his right hand with his good left hand and put it around the ring."

Both men suffered severe burns of the face and hands. Huff's clothing was smoldering as he left the plane. When the observer had jumped out, the pilot kept the burning plane in level flight until he heard Huff's parachute pop open. He knew then that his observer had cleared the burning pyre. What happened afterward was hazy in Goulding's mind. But he recalled that after his observer had begun his descent, the pilot slid his seat back as far as it would go, turned himself sideways in it after unfastening his safety belt, and kicked the stick forward and to the left as he jumped. Goulding began pulling at his rip cord the minute he left the plane. But he stopped himself until he had cleared the aircraft, as visions of colliding with the blazing L-19 crossed his mind. When he finally yanked the D-ring to open his umbrella, the doomed aircraft had begun a lazy spiral away from him.

It was the first jump for both officers, but neither remembered any sensations as their parachutes opened. The wind drifted them to a landing 300 yards apart in front of the infantry outposts of the Korean Marine Division. They were picked up by friendly patrols after they had untangled themselves from the parachutes' shroud lines. The airmen were evacuated that night to a mobile army surgical hospital after receiving first aid. Both men were then taken to a hospital in Japan. Due to skillful open-air treatment of their wounds by Army medics, neither man will bear unsightly scars of his experience. Huff, who was due for rotation to the States, was sent home. He had flown 73 combat missions as a volunteer artillery air observer. He had been on the thirteenth mission above the limit of 60 he had set for himself. Goulding returned to flying duty with the Korea Military Advisory Group. Both men were later awarded the Silver Star for the gallantry with which they had conducted themselves in this action.

In the meanwhile, a new aircraft appeared in Korea. On 22 December, the first L-20 DeHavilland Beaver, a multi-place, all-metal, ton-carrying, 450 horsepower aircraft was delivered. With this plane, Army Aviators went into the "Pee Wee Airlines" business. Brought over on an aircraft carrier

The new DeHavilland "Beaver" L-20 plane prepared to take off on a demonstration flight at an airstrip in Korea, with Major General Williston B. Palmer, CG, X Corps, aboard.   (U. S. Army Photo)

to Japan by Captain Guy C. Meiss of Nescopeck, Pennsylvania, the Beaver (number 6266) made the rounds of the battlefront to be shown to Army Aviators and to ground commanders. Demonstrated were the capabilities of the aircraft for carrying combat cargo, or five passengers, or two litter patients and an aid man, or for making cargo drops from its wing shackles or through a well in its fuselage. The first plane was assigned to the Eighth Army Flight Detachment, with subsequent deliveries going to the Corps and Divisions on the front.

After four months of winter operation in Korea, the Beaver had fulfilled a mechanic's dream for the ease with which it could be maintained under difficult operating conditions. M/Sgt. James O. Goodwin of Wilmington, California, the crew chief of 6266 who had accompanied the aircraft on its long voyage to Japan aboard the Navy carrier USS Windham Bay, was enthusiastic about its performance.

"Maintenance? There just isn't any," he was prone to say. Goodwin pointed out that the only difficulty experienced with the Beaver had been with brake clips which were in short supply.

"The brake clips holding the friction disc in place are easily lost. Replacing them is a simple job, but the difficulty comes in getting an adequate supply of them." This problem was overcome by the 79th Ordnance which began the manufacture of the parts at Ascom City.

The popular feature of the L-20, as far as the mechanics were concerned, was the cold-weather starting characteristic of the plane. An oil dilution system built into the aircraft allowed easy starting on battery alone, even on mornings of 11 degrees below zero. The working of this system was simple. At the end of each winter day's flight, a switch was flipped to activate a fuel pump which forced gasoline into the oil system of the aircraft engine. The gasoline kept down the viscosity of the oil during the cold night so that easy starting in the early morning run-up could be accomplished without having first to thaw the oil. All of the gasoline injected into the oil system would be boiled out during the first 30 minutes the engine was run up the next day.

The Beaver was a worthy partner in the Army Aviation team. Its years of faithful service in the bush country of Alaska and Canada had resulted from the modifications and improvements suggested by its bush pilots and incorporated by its builders.

General James A. VanFleet, Eighth Army commander, rewarded the services of his personal pilot, Capt. Bruce O. Ihlenfeldt, with the Bronze Star Medal. (U. S. Army Photo)

CHAPTER 7

UNTIL TRUCE
DO US PART

The "Van Fleet Weather" legend grew during the first winter of General James A. Van Fleet's tenure as Eighth Army commander. Captain Bruce O. Ihlenfeldt of Lawton, Oklahoma, flew Van Fleet for five months in Korea. His story best described the legend: *

> "In November 1951, I flew General Van Fleet for the first time in the L-19 (number 50-1418) which he used as an aerial jeep. With another pilot of the Eighth Army Flight Detachment, I took my L-19 to Taegu where we picked up the General and President Syngman Rhee of the Republic of Korea. It was during this trip that I had my first insight into the man I was to fly across the length and breadth of the United Nations zone during the next five months.

> "We landed our planes in a town not far from Taegu. The airstrip was situated near a Korean school and about 100 children were on hand to greet us. Van Fleet asked me if we had any candy. Since the General's plane always carried a stock of chocolate bars, I got out a box and handed it to him. As he opened it, he was mobbed by the children. Van Fleet held the box above his head, and in an attempt to clear himself of the youngsters who were climbing his tall, solidly-built frame, he threw several of the candy bars to the outer fringes of the crowd. President Rhee, meanwhile, had come to the rescue when Van Fleet was mobbed, but his efforts to pull off the friendly attackers were in vain. Van Fleet's strategy in throwing candy bars one by one diverted the interest of most of the children as they scattered to claim their loot.

> "I was unsuccessful at hiding my amusement at this turn of events. But I learned from this first experience that even in such a small-scale engagement Van Fleet could apply tactics as he had learned them in his 41 years of Army service.

*By permission, VFW Magazine.

"Many persons ask how I came to inherit the job of flying Van Fleet. I had begun flying light aircraft in 1938. I had logged more than 6,000 hours of flying time as a Civilian Pilot Training instructor back in Springfield, Illinois; as a civilian flight instructor at the Air Training Department at Fort Sill, Oklahoma; and as senior check pilot for Army Aviation students there. They tell me that I was chosen for the job because I happened to be the most experienced Army Aviator in Korea. I had just finished a six-months' combat tour with the 2nd Inf. Div. aviation section when I was appointed to the job.

"But when you fly for a General, it seems to me that experience alone is not enough to do a good job. The faith must be built up in the passenger that the pilot has learned from the experience to which he has been exposed. I think that the greatest tribute to my capabilities which Van Fleet has given me has been the ease with which he travels by air. I have always found him calm and uncommunicative while in flight.

"Pilots of the Eighth Army Flight Detachment, which is the transportation unit for staff personnel in Korea, have had reason to add to the meteorologists' classifications of weather conditions. They have accepted the weatherman's word when he dubs existing conditions as CAVU (ceiling and visibility unlimited), VFR (visual flight rules apply), Marginal, or IFR (instrument flight rules apply). But they have added another which they term 'Van Fleet Weather'. This description of weather conditions has arisen because of the unfortunate affinity which the General has had for the unusual on the weather menu. Some bomber pilots have been known to be definitely 'jinxed' by attracting flak. Van Fleet seems to attract unusual weather, most of it bad.

"When Cardinal Spellman made a tour of the fighting front on Christmas Eve, 1951, I flew Van Fleet in the group of airplanes which made up the 'rat race', as we dubbed such mass flights carrying VIP's (very important persons) on fast inspection tours. We had dropped the Cardinal and his party at X Corps headquarters on the northeastern front where he was to conduct services for the troops the next day. I then had flown the General back to his headquarters in Seoul. Christmas Day dawned with a cold rain drizzling in freezing temperature which was ideal for wing icing. At 0830 hours, an

L-19 landed at our airstrip after a short 15-minute flight. The pilot had turned back after picking up a half-inch of ice on his wings which had so affected his lift as to make flying hazardous. After checking with airstrips by telephone throughout the peninsula, I found that flying had been curtailed for Army aircraft because of the icing conditions. I then called Van Fleet's office and informed his aide of the inadvisability of the flight. I was supported in this by Lt. Col. J. Elmore Swenson, the Eighth Army's aviation officer. When the General came out, however, he insisted on flying to his meeting with the Cardinal.

"I took off with misgivings, since I felt a great responsibility in exposing the General to the dangerous weather conditions. As I listened to radio transmissions throughout our flight, I became more and more uneasy. Army pilots from one coast to the other were calling in distress notices for emergency landings. Since it was inevitable that I make the flight, I watched the free air temperature gauge very closely and changed my altitude frequently so that I would be flying through the valleys where the warmest levels of air could be found. We made our destination without picking up any ice. This was a feat which I later discovered was not duplicated by any other Army pilot on the peninsula that day. Van Fleet was able to rejoin the Cardinal for Christmas, but Mother Nature still had the last word, for a blinding snowstorm grounded our aircraft for the following two days.

"Another incident about Van Fleet weather made the rounds of military circles in Korea in January 1952.

"We had taken off from a frontline Army airstrip under threatening skies in the west central sector. In about 15 minutes we found ourselves in a blinding snow squall. Knowing that the General was anxious to return to his headquarters for the night, I continued southward in hopes that the squall was only a local condition which would improve. I had made a mental note of the location of an abandoned airstrip over which we had flown, however. When I could no longer see the ground, I made a quick reversal of direction and headed back for the emergency strip, where I was able to land in the two inches of snow which had fallen. As I was making the turn, Van Fleet, who had been silent throughout the flight, remarked in a calm voice: 'We passed over a strip back there.'

"The General and his aide, Colonel F. T. Mildren of Las Vegas, Nevada, who had been following us in a second L-19 flown by Lt. Wilbur J. Pennypacker of Lewistown, Pennsylvania, walked to the road near the airstrip. The General flagged down an approaching jeep driven by a young Lieutenant with a cigarette dangling from his lips.

"'What the hell do you want?' the Lieutenant yelled.

"Without a word, Van Fleet pushed back the hood of his parka to reveal four gleaming silver stars. The Lieutenant, I recall, tried to get out of his jeep to come to attention and brace himself for a salute as he tried to get rid of his cigarette, all in one fast movement.

"The General smiled as he mounted the jeep for his ride back to headquarters.

"Flying Van Fleet in Korea has been an interesting job. I have had the opportunity of seeing at close range such internationally famous persons as the 'Veep', Mrs. Anna Rosenberg, General J. Lawton Collins and General Matthew B. Ridgway. I have found all of them most affable. General Ridgway, for example, had always shown his appreciation for the efforts of Army Aviators by presenting them with boxes of Whitman's Sampler chocolates after a flying tour of inspection of the Korean front.

"Van Fleet likes the L-19 aircraft best of those which are used in Army Aviation. He feels that the most desirable characteristic for the passenger is the excellent visibility which it affords. The General is an excellent air traveller. He is always oriented, and even without using a map he has reminded me when I have strayed as much as an eighth of a mile off course. Van Fleet knows the peninsula so well that he can recount in great detail the specific actions which have taken place in any sector since he assumed command of the Eighth Army.

"I have flown Van Fleet in an L-19 from east coast to west, and from Koje-do in the south to Kumwha on the northern front. And because of his even temperament, I have found him easier to fly than many officers of lesser rank. The only time I ever saw Van Fleet wear earphones to listen to radio transmissions was the day

I received a call from Lt. Wayne J. Miller of Crystal Springs, Mississippi, that he was losing oil pressure. Miller was carrying one of the General's aides as passenger. When I informed the General of the situation, he put on his earphones to listen as Miller kept me posted, as flight leader, of the condition of his aircraft. He finally made it back to our home base with no trouble.

"The only time in my experience with Van Fleet when he preferred to take the train back to Seoul because of weather conditions was during a 'rat race' with General Ridgway. Snow squalls and icing were on order that day, too. But the UN Commander overrode Van Fleet's dissuasions by saying: **'Let's go take a look, Van.** If it isn't any good, we can come back and take the train.' As it happened, Van Fleet agreed reluctantly and we were able to get back to Seoul all right. But I can still remember the basis for the General's desire to take the train. As we climbed into our plane, he said: 'I wouldn't hesitate to fly if it were just us. But I am responsible for him.'

"And that's the way I feel about my job."

Just before the new year was ushered in, Lt. James F. Reed of Tulsa, Oklahoma, sank a tank. During a routine mission, Reed sighted an enemy tank crossing a frozen river in the east sector. He directed the firing of three artillery rounds which bracketed the tank, broke the ice covering the river and caused the tank to sink. The airman, who had been hovering low over his target for an hour, radioed his base: "Sighted tank, sank same." He received the Distinguished-Flying Cross for this action.

Army Aviation joined the Navy in January 1952 to participate in shore-to-hospital-ship evacuation of wounded. The project was conducted as an experiment with the helicopters of the Air Force, Marines and the Army. Each branch of the armed services used its particular types of aircraft and specialized techniques. Two H-13D (Bell) Army helicopters were used by the Army during its phase of the experiment. One was stationed ashore and the other aboard the USS Consolation which was anchored 12 miles north of the 38th Parallel off the east coast. Under the command of Captain Grover C. Trumbo of Birmingham, Alabama, the Army operations proved so successful that recommendation was made to the Navy Department that the Army's helicopter and operating techniques be adopted.

The experiment began on 9 January when the 8192nd Helicopter Detachment, attached to the 8209th MASH in northeastern Korea, was chosen to represent the Army. For twelve days beginning 12 January, four pilots and one enlisted mechanic were instrumental in transferring about 150 critically wounded UN soldiers without even a minor mishap.

In a typical mission, a helicopter was flown off a clearing company airstrip on the beach with the patients in each of two litters on either side of the craft. Personal gear of the patients was carried in the cockpit. The trip to the Consolation took about five minutes and was usually flown at about 100 feet over the water. Two helicopters were on duty at the same time. One was kept on shore to pick up patients, while the other remained on the flight deck of the hospital ship. When the helicopter on shore took off with its load of patients, its sister ship took off from the flight deck of the Consolation to land at the shore base for the next load. Most of the patients to be taken out to the hospital ship had arrived at the shore base by air transport from airfields scattered throughout the eastern sector of the UN zone in Korea. They were brought to the hospital ship for specialized treatment which was not available at shore installations. The greatest number of patients to be evacuated in a single day was 42. This number was high, considering the stability of the fighting front during the period of the evacuation experiment.

The Consolation had been equipped with a 60 x 60 foot landing platform on the stern of the ship. A total of 18 Navy men was assigned to handle the aerial operation. These included a flight deck officer who gave hand signals to the helicopter pilot making a landing, a radio officer who maintained contact with the aircraft for landings and takeoffs, a seaman who maintained contact with the ship's bridge through the intercom system, a doctor and corpsman who received the patients as they were landed on the ship, five plane handlers who stood by with firefighting equipment, and four men in a crash boat which patrolled the waters close to the ship for rescue operations in the event of accidents.

In his report on the experiment, Captain Trumbo said that no specialized helicopter training for pilots in on the operation was necessary:

> "There's no difference in flying the helicopter to a flight deck than there is to a land strip," he said, "excepting that the pilot must watch the flight deck officer instead of the deck. If the pilot watches the deck, he

might pitch the helicopter with the roll of the ship to try and keep the helicopter level with the landing deck."

Maintenance of the helicopters used in the experiment was handled on shore. But a mechanic, Sgt. Norman Kessler of Champagne, Illinois, was stationed on the Consolation to take care of emergency repairs. Fortunately, no mechanical difficulties were experienced during the operation. Batteries were removed from the helicopter at night, however, to keep them charged during the cold weather.

All the patients who were brought to the Consolation were seriously wounded UN soldiers who needed care which could only be provided by a general hospital. Transported on standard litters, the patients who were conscious of their surroundings showed great interest in their first helicopter rides.

"The flights took such a short time that I never knew any of the patients I was flying," Captain Trumbo said. "But it was a good feeling to know that their short five minutes with me was another important link which contributed to their speedy recovery."

On return trips to shore, the helicopters transported patients who were well enough to be sent to hospitals in Japan and the States. The greatest shore-bound load was 17 men in 35 minutes on one occasion. This evacuation would have taken at least two hours if the patients had been taken by small boat to shore, then by ambulance to the air evacuation planes waiting at the airstrip. Administrative flights were also made by the Army helicopters. Cases of blood plasma were transported to the hospital ship as they were delivered by air courier at the shore strip. And when the sea was too rough for a small boat, the "whirlybird" was used to carry personnel, mail and movies to and from the shore.

That the experiment was a success was indicated by Captain John W. McElroy of Quincy, Massachusetts, the commander of the Consolation, in a letter to Captain Trumbo.

"This record (the transfer of approximately 150 patients) verifies my opinion that the assignment of two of the H-13 type helicopters to a ship of this type anchored off shore from medical clearing stations greatly simplifies the transfer, evacuation and prompt medical care of patients, and should be contemplated in all future operations.

"Captain Trumbo and his group are to be congratulated on their record, and should serve as an example to any future operations of a similar nature. This command wishes to express its thanks for both the skill and operational efficiency of this group."

Other pilots taking part in the Consolation experiment were Lt. Basil Abbott of Burlington, Vermont; Lt. Thomas Blakeley of Seattle, Washington; and Captain Robert Williams of Eldorado, Texas.

The early months of the new year found the truce talks oscillating between the genuine desires for a cease-fire by the UN negotiators and the frustrating propaganda tirades of the Reds. The hopes and fears of the UN troops in Korea rose and fell with the Panmunjom barometer. The 155-mile front remained static. "Watch and wait" was maintained as the unofficial order of the day. Sporadic patrol actions by both sides punctuated the waiting. The final fighting line had been established generally along the real estate limits of 10 June 1951. On 24 January, General Ridgway announced that the truce talks had been stalemated by the Red demands for forcible repatriation of war prisoners. The next month, the talks were further endangered when on 18 February, the first of a series of prisoner riots broke out in the Communist's POW compounds on Koje-do, an island off the southern coast.

Meanwhile, Army air was continuing its activities on the front. On 18 February, the first real mystery of the war to be contributed by Army Aviation was enacted. Major Larry Loos, aviation officer of IX Corps Artillery, undertook a behind-the-lines G-2 mission with an Intelligence observer. The last radio contact with Loos was recorded at 1630 hours, after which he was neither heard from nor seen again. Searching aircraft found no trace of the missing plane. Aerial photos were taken of the area near Chorwon where he had last reported his position. The searchers found a hole in a frozen lake about eight miles behind the enemy lines which may have sealed his fate. The shape of the hole resembled one which might have outlined the crash of a small aircraft. Front line observers of the 2nd Division reported that Chinese soldiers had been fishing around the lake after the plane had been reported missing. But no concrete evidence of Loos' fate was ever established.

With the advent of more peaceful days in Korea, the Army began an all-out economy drive to conserve the taxpayers' cost of the war. Army Aviation took up the crusade and all its aircraft were marked with the initial cost and operating expense for all to see. The L-19 aircraft, for example, was labelled: "Cost - $13,000. Cost per hour - $15." This information was stencilled aft of the cockpit entrance on the right side of the fuselage so that passengers mounting the aircraft could not fail to be impressed. Since the information evoked few guilty consciences among junketing brass, one crew chief facetiously added this line: "Is this trip necessary?"

But Captain Charles N. Posz of Eau Claire, Wisconsin, made one of the most unusual contributions to cost consciousness on 24 February. During his eleventh combat mission since joining the 2nd Division Artillery, Posz, accompanied by Lt. Ralph T. Clark of Smithfield, Utah, was orbiting at an altitude of 6,000 feet above a suspected enemy position in the vicinity of Pyonggang near the "Iron Triangle" when his plane was hit by enemy ack-ack. His right wing lost about 12 square feet of surface from the painted star out-board. This was Clark's seventy-eighth mission as they turned tightly to the left while examining evidence of heavy traffic near a building six miles behind enemy lines. Despite the loss of part of his wing, Posz was able to regain control of his aircraft although it took a thousand feet of precious altitude and

CAPT. CHARLES N. POSZ *made one of the most unusual contributions to cost consciousness when he brought back for a safe landing his L-19 which had had twelve square feet of its right wing sheared off by enemy fire.*

a straight-down speed of 125 miles per hour. Posz found that when the aircraft was slowed to about 110 mph, it started to stall. So he kept Number 1632 going at full throttle as he headed southward toward friendly lines. To compensate for the loss of the right wing area, full left rudder and full left aileron had to be applied. And it took the combined strengths of both the pilot and observer to keep the ship in the air.

Capt. Charles N. Posz of Eau Claire, Wisconsin.

As soon as the plane had been righted after being hit, Clark sent out a trouble call over the radio. Lt. John J. Self of Lock Haven, Pennsylvania, another Second-to-None pilot flying a special mission in the same area with his observer, Lt. C. J. Wangerin of Utica, N. Y., answered the call. The stricken aircraft was experiencing radio difficulties so that only VHF contact with Self was feasible. Self, therefore, escorted his wing mate to Hartell Field, the 2nd Div. Arty. airstrip, where he acted as a relay station to the base control radio. When they reached the friendly lines, Posz turned to his observer.

"Clark, you bail out," he said.
"What are you going to do, Posz?
"I'm going to try and bring it in."

Clark decided to stay with the ship. As he explained it later:

"The pressure on the controls was such that I knew it would take both of us to keep the thing in the air. Posz also needed someone to work the radio. And I wanted to stay for the ride."

At Hartell Field, Posz made three passes at the runway. He found that the L-19 could not be landed on the short strip at 110 mph. At slower speeds, he found that the lack of control became dangerous both for the occupants of the Army aircraft and for the personnel on the field should a landing be attempted.

Lt. Self relayed a message from Major Chester A. Dillahunt of Springfield, Ohio, the 2nd Division aviation officer:

"To hell with the ship, Posz. Get altitude and bail out."

After bringing the wounded aircraft that close to home, Posz and Clark were determined to make one more attempt at saving the plane. At the suggestion of Lt. Self, a bearing was taken to an Air Force field (K-47) at Chunchon, twenty minutes away. Captain Posz felt certain that 1632 could be landed safely and repaired to fly again against the enemy. Escorted by Self in his L-19 and followed by the Division's helicopter carrying a medic, the clipped-wing ship was flown eastward. Self contacted the Air Force tower at K-47 and requested assistance in bringing in the stricken plane. The airmen later lauded their sister organization for its cooperation during the emergency. When the flight arrived at the field, all aircraft had been warned away from the traffic pattern on a Mayday alert. All radio transmissions on the tower frequency had been silenced to other aircraft, the runway was cleared, a crash truck, fire truck and ambulance were standing by. Even a litter-equipped helicopter was made airborne to hover beside the L-19 as it staggered into the pattern and began its descent to safety.

"It was a great feeling to know that we had both the Army and the Air Force ready to help us that day," Posz said later. "It was a real team operation."

The plane was brought in at full throttle, with the airspeed indicator reading 135 mph. It took nearly all of the 4,600 feet of runway before the wheels stopped rolling and Captain Posz' private "operation salvage" was completed. But it took three airmen to do the job. The pilot insisted he could not have maintained control of the ship without the help of

Clark or Self in the second plane.

> "Self was right behind me and kept yelling instructions over the radio, advising me as to how I could keep control of my ship on the ground at our high landing speed."

The story did not end with the successful landing. Though the flight, from wing loss to landing, took only an hour, word of the L-19's predicament had spread along the front. One pilot who heard of it was several miles away from the Air Force field. He was Lt. Atley Gaddie of Oklahoma City, an Ordnance Army Aviator who had been picking up a wrecked plane. Much to Posz' surprise, Gaddie had a complete right wing ready to be installed on 1632 to replace the one which had been hit. Within three hours, Posz' plane was ready to be flown out to an Ordnance unit (OLAM) for more complete repairs. Installing the new wing were Sgt. Andrew Biro of Alton, Illinois, and Corporal James Storm of Denver, Colorado. Both men were with the 45th OLAM.

Captain Posz, a former flight instructor for Army Aviators at Fort Sill, Oklahoma, flew his newly repaired plane out of Chunchon. But he did it alone, following an unwritten rule among Army Aviators that "if you crack up a ship, get into another immediately and fly". But Posz got to fly his own ship.

Both men received the Distinguished Flying Cross for this action.

Posz became the only Army Aviator in anyone's memory to receive the award of two DFC's within a six-day period. On 1 March, he won the cluster to his DFC of 24 February by assisting an infantry team to rescue the crews of two UN tanks which had been disabled by enemy mines. The citation for this award read:

> "On the morning of 1 March 1952, Captain Posz, flying a light, unarmed aircraft, was engaged in directing artillery and mortar supporting fire against strongly fortified enemy positions (in the vicinity of Yongho-dong) which were undergoing attack by a friendly infantry unit. Flying at extremely low altitudes through heavy enemy fire, he observed two friendly tanks become disabled by hostile mines. Seeing that the rescue parties sent to recover the vehicles and lead their crews to safety were pinned down by heavy enemy fire, Captain Posz, without regard for his personal

safety, began making repeated passes over the hostile
positions within a few feet of the ground. His courage-
ous actions diverted the foe's attention long enough for
the friendly rescue parties to carry out their mission."

The war may have been nearly over to Stateside civilians who
had lost interest in the Korea "police action", but it was very
real to the combat soldiers in the bunkers and cockpits.

CHAPTER 8

ROTATION REVERIES

By the time January 1952 had rolled around on the Army
Aviation front, all of the pioneers of the first months of fighting had been rotated to Japan or Stateside assignments. Replacements poured into Korea in greater numbers than ever
before as recalled Reservists, National Guardsmen, newly-
trained pilots and Stateside "carpet baggers" flowed through
the pipeline. A rotation system of one year's service in
Korea had been established. This period normally included
six months in a combat unit and six months in the rear.

Demands for the services of Army Aviators by ground commanders in increasing varieties of missions resulted in the
presence of about 350 pilots flying in the theater by the end
of the year. This was a far cry from the few airmen who had
flown the first missions during the terrible weeks after the
outbreak of war.

The times became trying for the UN troops engaged in the
"police action". It was determined that one soldier out of
every seven was actually under fire in the bunkers. The
others were needed to back him up along the supply channels
to the rear. Army Aviation's manpower pie was cut a little
finer. For each flyer in a combat unit, there was one pilot
in a "rear" assignment.

Regardless of the airman's assignment, the problem of morale was ever present. The Army Aviators "sweated out"
their last missions on the front and their replacements from
the States. The major anticipations of a pilot's existence
were hinged on the letter "R". Little "R" and Big "R" colored
the dreams and plans of Army Aviators all over the peninsula. Little "R" was his rotation from the uncertainties of
front line flying; Big "R" was his rotation to home, or "Truman's Island", as he called it. In between these extremes
of "R" was "R&R", rest and recuperation leave in Japan
which was extended periodically.

The three R's for the airmen provided lighter moments.

The grapevine in Korea informed a combat veteran of the coming of his replacement, even to his full name and service number. There was a ceremony connected with the exchange of status. Take the case of Smith coming in for Jones as an example. Smith had been greased through the pipeline for a hasty voyage by air to Korea. He landed in Taegu where he was already expected because O'Flaherty had checked on arrivals at Camp Drake near Tokyo during his last R&R a few days previously. O'Flaherty had brought the glad tidings to his unit, which had known that Jones was next on the list for Big "R". Jones was informed by the grapevine that his replacement was due in. He immediately began a schedule of telephone calls to Taegu. These were climaxed when Smith reported for duty. If Jones could swing a flight to Taegu, almost 300 miles from his unit, he would hot-foot it down there to bring back his replacement, bag and baggage. If he couldn't make the trip himself, he haunted the EUSAK courier base at Seoul until his replacement showed up. Then it would be a matter of minutes before Smith would be bedded down in Jones' sack which by custom he inherited, along with the comfort items which Jones had collected during his year in Korea. Such impedimenta might include partly-filled bottles of duty and tax-free spirits, hospital bed sheets laboriously bartered from a nearby MASH in exchange for air transportation, or a voltage regulator purchased on an early R&R in Japan to step up the electric current so that a prized portable radio might be tuned to the Armed Forces Radio Service stations. Jones had long before learned the truth of the adage that "He who travels lightest travels farthest", so that his home-bound baggage might be depleted to the extent that he bequeathed upon Smith his odds and ends of Army-issued clothing, especially a flying suit which was an item in short supply. Or it might be a flying jacket, or a shoulder holster, or shoepacks, or even a Marilyn Monroe calendar. Whatever it was, Smith took the item for bartering purposes if for no other.

Jones took good care of his replacement right up until the time his orders were received for the Big "R". He made sure that Smith negotiated all stairways in safety, that he did not strain himself by carrying his own baggage, that he did not fall ill and so require hospitalization. Such a catastrophe might mean delays for Jones in his trip to the States.

As soon as his replacement took over the veteran's duties, Jones would pack his one B-4 bag and pause long enough at the pilots' sign-out board to mark his destination: "Truman's Island".

With Jones departure from the "Land of the Morning Calm" he might also leave the gripes which he had exchanged on innumerable occasions with his fellow "Flyboys". Of necessity, the majority of the flyers in Korea were recalled Reserve Officers, many of whom had served in the combat airlanes of World War II. Adding to the bitterness which they had experienced in being recalled for a "police action" was their discovery that the old World War II Army Aviation problems still flickered. Promotions were few and inter-service jealousies were many.

Army Aviators had always been in a peculiar position in the Army because they did a specialized job as members of organizations whose commanders, for the most part, had little understanding for their work. The fact that they received incentive pay for their dangerous work was often a bone of contention. Because of the lack of understanding of their problems in carrying out their flying missions, many times the Army Aviators found themselves subjected to unreasonable demands for performance. The lack of coordination of the Army Aviation operation on staff level often resulted in confusion. Many times the flyers were chastised for not having aircraft available for administrative flights even though the planes were all tied up on the combat missions which they rightly considered to be of foremost consideration. They became resentful when some ground commanders duplicated air missions unnecessarily.

Army Aviators in one front line sector may still be chuckling ironically over their division commander's order that each day a light plane was to fly at low altitude over the friendly front line positions. The explanation given was that such missions would provide a morale uplift for the ground troops by showing them that their "eyes" were always open above them, watching out for enemy movements. But what the commander had failed to understand was that flying low over the MLR (main line of resistance) exposed the Army Aviators to the trajectories of friendly mortar and artillery firing, as well as to enemy small arms fire. During World War II, this tactic had worked, since the Germans had respected the little planes and had taken cover when they appeared. As General Van Fleet later pointed out:

> "If one of our World War II infantry groups found itself under German artillery fire, it called for either counterbattery fire or a Cub plane. Either was enough to silence the German guns. The Germans conserved their guns and crews, and never wanted to give away

their positions. One little Cub plane was enough to stop their fire; we sent Cubs up time after time and they never failed. "

But this was a new war with different tactics. The Reds were reckless in firing at the little planes, so that missions at high altitudes, out of range of enemy small arms, became standing operating procedure for Army Aviation.

Fortunately, only a scattering of interference by ground commanders was experienced in the selection of airstrips as bases of operation. For almost the entire decade during which Army Aviation had been organic to the Army, the ill-advised propaganda that the light planes could land on a post-age stamp had plagued its pilots. For ground commanders in many instances had based their judgments on this theory when they had demanded that the light plane strips be established in restricted areas on the very doorsteps to their command posts. Fortunately, the coming of the helicopter did a lot to satisfy the commanders' whims in this respect. But insofar as the fixed-wing operations were concerned, it took the loss of plane and pilot in some instances to prove to a ground commander that atmospheric conditions, as well as those of terrain, are those factors which decide the situation of an airstrip from which flight operations can be conducted in safety.

One division artillery commander in Korea insisted that his airstrip be located adjacent to his CP in a valley which was under enemy observation from a height only a couple of miles away. Even after a period of shelling, the commander remained adamant when it was suggested that the air installation be moved three miles to the rear where the division air section was based. When he discovered, however, that no replacement aircraft would be provided should any be destroyed by enemy shelling, the move was effected.

By the second anniversary of Korea, the Air Force-Army Aviation rift had closed considerably. The cleavage between the services had widened earlier as the Army air service had expanded away from the Air Force claim that all flying equipment should be its "baby". But a new enemy had appeared in the form of inter-arm and service jealousies within the Army itself. The most significant of these was between the infantry and artillery aviation sections. The artillery almost invariably flew six combat missions to every one flown by the infantry sections. The artillery missions were longer, often lasting from two and one-half to four and one-half hours;

while the infantry missions lasted mostly the one hour required for them to be logged as combat missions. Many infantry sections had 11 pilots who were sent out on missions whose variety ranged from combat reconnaissance to administrative flights to the rear areas. They were able to fly every other day. The artillery pilots, on the other hand, usually numbering ten for duty, flew every day, two missions a day. Where the maximum flying time for the infantry pilots had averaged about 70 hours a month, the average for the artillery pilots had reached more than 100 hours a month. Yet, the R&R frequency for both sections was the same: every 6 to 12 weeks. Another resentment arose from the fact that when a division went into reserve, the artillery section continued its combat missions in support of units which remained on the front. The infantry air sections, on the other hand, took on as their principal tasks the flying of administrative missions. Despite these discrepancies, the combat tour remained six months for each.

The position of the Army Aviation officer had always been innocuous. He had been placed in an advisory position, but his advice was rarely sought, or taken. He found himself to be the go-between of inter-service bickering. Many artillery commanders insisted upon exercising control over the artillery planes, as did the infantry commanders. The Signal Corps insisted that pilots of that branch fly its planes. Actually, the only service which had a legitimate argument that branch-qualified officers fly its planes has been the Ordnance Corps. Every pilot, regardless of branch of service, had received the same type of training and was qualified to do any job, excepting Ordnance, required of Army Aviators. It does not take a Signal Corps pilot to fly message center runs; nor the artillery pilot to carry an observer to adjust fire. As a result, the Army Aviation officer attempting to establish centralized control of Army aircraft within a division to effect the most efficient and economical use of men and material had been frustrated at every turn in Korea. That centralization could work for the benefit of all concerned was proved in at least two divisions which experimented with this concept in Korea. The results of such centralization were that the pilots suffered less fatigue with the equalization of the combat flying load, less duplication of missions made for more efficient operation, and greater economy of aircraft maintenance resulted.

The problem of promotions was a delicate subject among Army Aviators. Despite an overstrength of Captains in Korea, a number of promotions in that grade were achieved for Army Aviators who had had a minimum of experience, but who happened to be "in the right place at the right time". Others in the theater who had had two-war experience as pilots were overlooked. Many pilots trained in grades higher than company rank were given section leadership for which they showed themselves singularly unqualified. Only in a few instances were appropriate steps taken to remedy this critical situation. And then only after the situation had become obviously untenable. By the end of the second year in Korea, Army Aviation was just beginning to reap the bitter harvest of its Topsy-like growth which had demanded ready-made rank so that its bargaining powers could be exercised on a negotiable level with ground commanders.

Especially during the period of stalemate in Korea, the uneconomical use of aircraft placed a burden upon the aircraft and the pilot. The equipment they used was never in completely tip-top shape because of the operating difficulties in Korea. This resulted in some resentment. But the situation gained great improvement during the later months under the efficient leadership of Lt. Col. J. Elmore Swenson, Eighth Army aviation officer, whose constant battle with supply agencies finally paid off.

The feeling among Army Aviators persisted that they were "orphans", in the sense that the very nature of their operations made them a group apart. This was in spite of the fact that there were many manifestations from the higher "brass" that the infant service was greatly appreciated as an integral part of the Army team. Some of the disservices done to Army commanders and Army Aviators alike by highly-placed staff officers unfortunately inspired confusion which gave some basis for the flyers' attitude. Some of these staff officers were flyers who had been placed in positions where they excused their own inadequacies by condemning the attitudes of "unreasonable" commanders who had not been properly educated in the mission and capabilities of Army Aviation. Other staff officers were in positions where they spoke for high commanders, even when their words would not have been authorized by their superiors, had they known of them. The situation was not new, either to the Army or to Army Aviation. But it was highly accentuated at this time because of the "police action" type of operation in Korea and because the existing situation was spread more thickly over a very small organization.

In spite of the many problems which had accompanied the Army Aviation operations in Korea, this unique service was able to play an important part in every event of historical importance which took place on the beleaguered peninsula. From the first landings of UN troops a few days after the NK forces had driven down from the north, to the uncertain days of the "peace" talks and the rotation "blues", Army Aviation continued its silent operations, largely unknown and conspicuously unsung.

The "postage stamp" landing areas of World War II have gone by the board in Korea, with engineer-built strips dotting the landscape. Here, at X Corps headquarters strip in the northeast sector, PFC Gerald L. Wood of Limwood, Michigan, "talks in" a light plane in the traffic pattern. (*U. S. Army Photo*)

CHAPTER 9

THE FIRST DECADE

The year 1952 found the Army Aviators celebrating their tenth anniversary as part of the Army team.

Under the leadership of Colonel Swenson, the first class of students had reported to the newly-established ROK Army Aviation school at Kwangju. Twenty Korean student officers with 50 hours of elementary flight training behind them had appeared for 80 to 90 hours of tactical flying, 100 hours of supervised evening study, and half-days of ground school instruction in aviation technical and mechanical subjects for a period of nine weeks. The school was under the supervision of Major Conway Ellers of Butte, Montana, assisted by Major John Givens of Abilene, Texas, and a staff of three US instructors. The objective of the school was to produce 100 pilots for the ROK Army. This project was to bear such

fruit that by the end of the war, the aim of the program was realized to provide eight pilots and seven aircraft per ROK division. Its success in this mission was best described by Colonel Swenson when he said:

> "The ROK officers were taken wringing wet from the rice paddies and within six months, they were developed into good flyers."

In appreciation of Swenson's efforts in making provisions for the ROKA participation in a vitally needed Army Aviation program, President Syngman Rhee presented this officer with the Ulchi Distinguished Service Medal of 11 March. The citation read, in part:

> "(His) distinctive ability and diplomacy in maintaining harmonious relations with the Republic of Korea and United Nations proved of marked international significance and contributed in high measure to the United Nations campaign in Korea."

On 22 March, the "Dragon Flight" celebrated its first anniversary. This unique organization had been dubbed the "VIP Airlines", for among its notable passengers had been Vice President Alben Barkley, Secretary of the Army Pace, Mrs. Anna Rosenberg, Generals of the Army Douglas MacArthur, Omar Bradley and George C. Marshall, Generals Van Fleet, Matthew B. Ridgway, Mark W. Clark and J. Lawton Collins; Field Marshal Earl Alexander of Great Britain, General Thrasivolos Tsakilatos of Greece, Admiral C. Turner Joy, Francis Cardinal Spellman, President and Mrs. Syngman Rhee, Screen Stars Betty Hutton, Jack Benny, Jennifer Jones, William Holden and Errol Flynn; Governor Thomas E. Dewey, Cartoonist Bill Mauldin, News Commentator Cedric W. Foster and LIFE Photographer Margaret Bourke-White. Passengers later in the year were to include President-elect Dwight D. Eisenhower and Radio-TV man Edward R. Murrow. Also to be listed on the flight log would be Secretary of Defense Wilson, Attorney General H. G. Brownell and the new Secretary of the Army Stevens.

In a letter of congratulations sent to Major Gerald H. Shea of Carmel, California, the unit commander, General Van Fleet wrote:

> "Your untiring efforts and conscientious devotion to duty during your first year of operations have provided this command with fast and efficient air transportation,

much of which was accomplished over hazardous terrain and under marginal weather conditions. This efficient service was all the more enhanced by the very enviable safety and maintenance records you achieved during the 8, 227 missions flown.

"I am proud of the significant contribution made by your officers and men, and am confident that it will do much toward favorably influencing the future status of Army Aviation. "

The lull in combat operations permitted Army Aviation to apply its energies to a variety of pursuits. One of these was the assignment by Colonel Swenson of Lt. Dario Politella of Kent, Ohio, a professional newspaperman, as information officer for Army Aviation in Korea. This was the first time that a PIO had been designated for Army Aviation in the field. For ten months, dispatches were filed from the peninsula carrying the dateline "WITH ARMY AVIATORS IN KOREA". The stories were disseminated to news agencies, newspapers and magazines. "Operation Prop Wash", as this venture was called, supplied 15, 000 words of news copy and 30, 000 words of magazine feature material; 24 separate radio shows were coordinated for the Far East and Stateside networks; material was coordinated for three Stateside television shows; a full-length motion picture, "This Is Army Aviation", was directed and the scenario written for filming by Signal Corps Photographer Joseph Kornfeld of Brooklyn; and technical direction was supplied for the filming of "Mission Over Korea" by Columbia Studios. This activity resulted in the award of the Bronze Star Medal to Lt. Politella on 20 October 1952.

One of the stories which was shared with the public was the experience of Lt. Wayne J. Miller of Crystal Springs, Mississippi, on 6 March.

"WITH ARMY AVIATORS IN KOREA... An Army Aviator of the 8th Army Flight Detachment flew a 'pigeon' to the east central front recently and came back to his base with a sparrow.

"Lt. Wayne J. Miller of Crystal Springs, Miss., was selected to fly the 'pigeon', a female war correspondent of a Hawaiian newspaper, to a front line unit. After dropping his passenger, Lt. Miller made a return flight in his L-19 Army aircraft to his home base.

"As he flew his final approach into the Army airfield,

Lt. Miller was startled by the appearance of a sparrow which fluttered up to the windshield in front of him from a hiding place underneath the pilot's seat.

"The Army Aviator advanced throttle and gained altitude for a new try at landing the aircraft. The hitch-hiking sparrow, meanwhile, gave up in its attempt to bail out and fluttered aft to the baggage compartment. Upon reaching the ground, the sparrow was liberated by the flustered airman.

"'He must have enjoyed the ride more than I did,' Miller said. 'I had a job getting him out.'

"And his wing mates said: 'Leave it to Miller to get the bird.'"

Other Army Aviators at this time turned their boredom to constructive channels. Captain William H. Chaires of Jacksonville, Florida, for example, decided he would make the fly-filled April days more comfortable for his fellows at the 2nd Division aviation section near Chipori. He went after the night-patrolling Korean flies with the help of his mechanic, Pfc. Lloyd T. Cook of Ridge Farm, Illinois. Together they constructed a makeshift DDT spray rig for his L-19, "Reveille With Beverly". A 20-gallon metal drum was set behind the pilot's seat and filled with the standard five per cent DDT with kerosene base mix. Flexible tubing was extended from a petcock attached to the drum to each of the two exhaust stacks from the L-19's engine. The stacks were extended about a foot in length so that the spray would not coat the underside of the plane's fuselage. When the petcock leading from the drum of chemical was opened, the liquid flowed to the hot exhaust stacks where it became atomized and forced out in the form of a fog.

Chaires and Cook did their spraying close to the ground during the times when the wind was calm. The first appearance of a smoking "Beverly" caused quite a furor, Chaires said, and his Hooper rating mounted as pilots reported on the Army radio channel that he was afire.

The new front which Chaires and Cook had opened in the central sector had as its objective the annihilation of every last one of the enemy.

"We'll never negotiate a peace with this enemy," Chaires said. "We're out to get every last airborne insect in our area. And from the results we got right from the beginning, it looks like we have the weapon to do it. "

"Operation Flicker" came into being in April when Politella and Kornfeld teamed up to film "This Is Army Aviation" to portray the story of operations in the combat theater. A total of 6, 250 feet of film was exposed in six weeks' time on locations all over the peninsula. The film became the first feature-length motion picture on Army Aviation to be recorded in an active combat theater. The film was marked as Project SPX-118 and sent to the Signal Corps Photographic Center in New York for editing and dubbing in of sound. The picture covered every aspect of Army Aviation operations, from artillery spotting to DDT spraying to helicopter evacuations.

Meanwhile, on 8 May, General Mark W. Clark arrived in the Far East to succeed General Ridgway as commander-in-chief of the UN forces. On his first inspection trip of his troops in Korea, the "Dragon Flight" went all-out to keep things in the Army family and to make him feel at home. For his first flight in an L-19 in Korea, General Clark was assigned as his pilot, Lt. Melrose F. Clark of Salem, Ohio. Lt. Clark, a veteran Army Aviator who flew Piper Cubs in Europe during World War II, was not related to the General, but the coincidence of names was too good an opportunity to be passed over.

The arrival of General Clark in the Far East was cause for rejoicing among Army Aviators. During the entire history of the infant organization of the Army, the General had displayed great interest in its development. His sympathetic participation in Army Aviation operations in Europe during World War II had secured for him a place in the hearts of old-time Liaison Pilots. In the interim years before Korea, his support of Army Aviation had manifested itself in the elaborate experimental and development organizations which were maintained during his tenure as Chief of the Army Field Forces. One of the first investigations undertaken by the General upon his arrival in Tokyo concerned the public relations responsibilities of Army Aviation in making known the story of the activities of this unique organization to a relatively uninformed world. And for the first time, an Army Aviator was assigned a prominent place on the FEC staff to coordinate the personnel and supply needs of the Army Aviation units in Korea. This staff officer was Lt. Col. Jack L. Marinelli, who had served with General Clark in Italy and at Headquarters, Army Field Forces.

THE BIG THREE *of the Far East: General Mark W. Clark, General Matthew B. Ridgway, and General James A. VanFleet all used the army light planes in their tours of Korea.* (U. S. Army Photo)

Being in the right place at the right time proved to be an old Army saw which explained the success of a team of Army Aviators on the central front on 11 May.

An unidentified Army L-19 pilot was flying along the MSR northeast of Chunchon when he saw a two-and-a-half ton truck leave the road and roll over. The pilot radioed this information to his home base. Since he was carrying a doctor as a passenger, the airman landed his L-19 on the road and the doctor administered first aid to three Turkish UN soldiers who were injured in the accident. Meanwhile, the radioed call for help had been intercepted by Lt. Eugene Fody of Encino, California, an Army Aviator assigned to the IX Corps aviation section near Chunchon. He called for a helicopter from the 8193rd Helicopter Detachment at the 8076th MASH. Answering the call was Lt. James R. Knighton of Columbus, Georgia, who began a search for the scene of the accident. He was guided to the pick-up spot by the L-19 pilot talking over the Army radio channel. When Knighton had made his pick-up of two of the injured soldiers, he requested that a second helicopter be dispatched from his unit to carry back the third patient. Answering this call was Captain Louis Hamner, also of Columbus, Georgia. Within an hour, all three patients were being given efficient medical treatment.

Commenting on the speedy success of their mission, the "chopper" pilots said:

> "Those Turks were lucky that Army Aviation was in the right place at the right time."

Knighton acquired an affinity for this type of operation. On another occasion, he was flying his helicopter along the Pukhan River south of the Hwachon Reservoir when he saw a truck loaded with ROK soldiers catapulting over a bridge into the river bed 75 feet below. Knighton landed under the span on the river bed and picked up two of the most critically injured soldiers. He deposited them at his home base several miles away and enlisted the aid of Lt. Edward Zeigler of Philadelphia to bring in the remaining patients. Of the truck load of 15 ROK soldiers, eight had died instantly, one was able to walk, and six were evacuated by helicopter. The complete evacuation mission was accomplished in a matter of minutes. As the last patients were being evacuated by air, an ambulance rolled up to the scene.

Meanwhile, the fighting front had become a classroom for some soldiers. The school was established over enemy territory in L-19's of the 40th Inf. Div. by Captain William Peterson of Baltimore, Maryland. The Fortieth had replaced the 1st Cav. Div. early in the year. Students taking the 10-day course in aerial observation were small unit leaders whose ground missions called for the use of Army observation aircraft. Their training aids were enemy artillery and the North Korean real estate which took the place of contour maps.

During June, the efficiency of one division aviation officer was rewarded with the presentation of the Legion of Merit, one of the few ever awarded to an Army Aviator for similar duties. Decorated was Major William G. Hale of Columbia, S. C., for duty with the 7th Inf. Div. aviation section.

As part of their preparations for the celebration of the tenth anniversary of Army Aviation on 6 June, the airmen began a search for "Miss Army Aviation of 1952" who was to be the symbol of their tenth year as a fighting part of the Army team. Each member of the aviation sections in Korea was invited to submit the photographs and physical specifications of female members of his family, current or prospective. The entries were judged by three civilian photographer-correspondents covering the Korean war: James A. Healy of United Press; Thomas W. McClellan of Fox-Movietone and

George E. Sweers of the Associated Press. Their choice was Miss Sylvia A. Carmen of Santa Monica, California, a Canadian-born model who was the fiancee of Lt. King S. Morrison. The statistics which won the title for the 27-year-old Californian were: height, 5 ft. 5 and one-half inches; weight, 110 lbs.; bust, 34 inches; waist, 21 inches; hips, 33 inches; and auburn hair. Morrison described her complexion as "beautiful".

MISS ARMY AVIATION *of 1952 was Sylvia A. Carmen of Santa Monica, California.*

The tenth anniversary was celebrated in Korea with air shows, open house at the airstrips, a week-long series of radio programs originating at AFRS Vagabond in Seoul, and messages of congratulations from military leaders. In Seoul, the premiere showing of "This Is Army Aviation" was presented.

But as the festivities were prepared, the war continued. Lt. Richard Potts and his observer, Lt. Thaddeus Meler, of the 25th Division's 64th FA Bn. brought their plane back from a mission during which they were hit in the tail section by enemy flak.

The second anniversary of the Korean war also found the Army Aviators paying homage to those among them who had closed out their logs. The two-year operations of Army Aviation had resulted in the tally of 94,339 combat missions, 117,593 administrative missions, and the evacuation of 7,654 sick and wounded by helicopter. Ten pilots had been recorded as killed in action, with two missing in action.

The 2nd Div. Arty. were probably the first to keep alive the name of one of their most honored airmen by naming their airfield after him. Hartell Army Airfield does not exist in official Eighth Army literature. Nor is this designation familiar to any but a few, even in Army Aviation circles in Korea. But to the old-timers of the 2nd Div. Arty. aviation section, the name Hartell symbolizes the bravery of the men who flew the front lines day after day in light, unarmed, and unarmored aircraft.

Lt. Lee R. Hartell of Danbury, Connecticut, was the first artilleryman connected with Army Aviation in Korea to earn the Congressional Medal of Honor. Strangely enough, Hartell won the award for action on the ground only two weeks after spending seven months as an aerial observer. After he had logged 210 combat missions, including three at night, Hartell was relieved of his duties as aerial observer for the 15th FA Bn. and was returned to his outfit to "take a rest" as a forward observer.

Hartell had been in the Far East about 17 months when he was killed in action on 27 August 1951. As an air observer, he had logged 446:15 hours. During the "May Massacre", the airman from Connecticut had spent 111:25 hours in the air to help the 2nd Division account for the slaughter of 75,000 advancing Reds. The Massacre itself had only lasted for the last few days of the month, but Hartell had conducted a month-long operation of his own. Lt. Oscar T. Rains of Albuquerque, N. M., recalled how Hartell had trapped a Red battalion near the Hwachon Reservoir by blocking the pass with artillery fire. Then, when the Red advance was stopped, he adjusted with v. t. type ammunition and accounted for 300 of the enemy. Hartell was the first artilleryman to be awarded the CMH in Korea. Only 16 officers were given such honors by the Army during the entire war. Of these, nine were killed or missing in action. The citation accompanying his award described the bravery of this quiet, unassuming officer:

"1st Lt. Lee R. Hartell...distinguished himself by conspicuous gallantry and intrepidity above and beyond the call of duty in action on 27 August 1951 in the vicinity of Kobangsan-ni, Korea. On that date, Lieutenant Hartell was attached to a rifle company as forward observer. During the darkness of the early morning his company was attacked by a numerically superior enemy. During the first hour, the enemy succeeded in working in close to the company perimeter along its front and both flanks. Although he had no cover and was completely exposed to the intense small arms and automatic weapons fire which the enemy was pouring into the company position, Lieutenant Hartell remained at his radio and adjusted accurate and devastating fire on the enemy. When a group of the enemy, screaming and yelling 'Banzai', charged through the perimeter firing small arms and hurling grenades and coming within a few yards of his position, Lieutenant Hartell, with complete disregard for his own safety and utter disdain for the enemy activity, continued to call for fire and refused to resort to the use of his personal weapon for self-defense. When he was painfully shot through the hand he jammed the wounded hand up into the opposite armpit to check the flow of blood, grasped his microphone with his other hand and continued to adjust fire in a calm and efficient manner until he had the front of his company protected by a close-in wall of fire and the left flank covered in a similar manner, leaving only one flank open to enemy attacks. During the last few minutes of this action, the rifle company had practically exhausted its ammunition and the artillery fire broke up the attack just in time to save the company from being overrun and annihilated. Just before the enemy dispersed, when the situation was most critical, Lieutenant Hartell uttered his last words, 'Keep firing both batteries, I think they've got us.' He then fell mortally wounded. He never knew it, but his devotion to duty and the self-sacrifice in continuing his adjustment, despite his wound and the terrific enemy fire, caused two hundred casualties on the enemy force and gave the friendly company time to obtain a resupply of ammunition and maintain its defensive position which was critical to the entire division front..."

When news of the death of Hartell reached his buddies at the 2nd Div. Arty. airstrip, there was stunned silence. But there was little surprise. Hartell's final, heroic action seemed singularly appropriate to the nature of the man as the Army Aviation pilots and crewmen had known it during the seven

months he had lived and flown with them as an aerial observer. The highest military honor of the land was presented
to Hartell's wife on 23 January 1952. But the memory of
Hartell's heroic deed is preserved less conspicuously by the
airmen of the Second.

Shortly after Hartell's death there appeared in front of the
operations tent of the 2nd Div. Arty. air section a sign fashioned from the boards of a cast-off C-ration box. It was painted with an Artillery-red background as being appropriate for
the brave, bloody action which it symbolized. It read, simply:

HARTELL FIELD
in honor of
1st Lt. Lee R. Hartell
15th F. A. Bn.
KIA 27 Aug. 1951

Hartell's fellow airmen agreed after his death that wherever
the 2nd Div. Arty. aviation section established a base of operations, the home-made marker would claim the spot as a
memorial to his courage.

And long after the UN forces leave Korea, one small plot of
that mountainous country at Chipori will remain forever dedicated to the gallantry of two Army Aviators who gave their
lives on 23 June 1952 while acting as cover for an infantry
company of the 7th Division in the attack. The Army airstrip
of the 7th Inf. Div. was dedicated to the Memory of Major

William P. Hunt of Macon, Georgia, the division air officer, and Lt. Marvin S. Murphy of St. Petersburg, Florida, Army Aviator. The two pilots had volunteered for a fatal, low-level reconnaissance mission to provide observation in assisting the 31st Inf. Regt. attacking in the vicinity of Hill 400 in the west central sector. During their mission, the two airmen adjusted artillery and mortar fire against the enemy at dangerously low altitude. They were killed when their L-19 was knocked down by enemy fire.

HUNT—MURPHY AIR STRIP

DEDICATED IN THE MEMORY OF MAJOR WILLIAM P. HUNT, AIR OFFICER, 7th INF. DIV. AND 1st LT. MARVIN S. MURPHY, PILOT, KILLED IN ACTION 0610 HRS. 21 JUNE 1952, WHILE FLYING A SPECIAL TYPE RECONNAISSANCE MISSION, PATROL COVER AND THE ADJUSTMENT OF ARTILLERY AND MORTAR FIRE, FOR THE 31st INF. REGT OVER HILL 400 NEAR KUMHWA, KOREA.

The dedication of Hunt-Murphy airstrip on 3 July was one of the last acts of the Seventh's retiring commander, Maj. Gen. L. L. Lemnitzer. While parading troops of the infantry regiments and division artillery and elements of the 73rd Tank Battalion passed in review, six aircraft flew formation overhead in salute to the brave airmen. General Lemnitzer told his command that the two Army Aviators had set a new standard for gallantry which he expected the Division to live up to in the future. A five-man squad fired three volleys and taps was sounded after the unveiling of a wooden plaque which would later be replaced by a bronze plaque set in concrete as a permanent marker for the airfield.

During the colorful dedication ceremonies, the combat missions of the air sections were uninterrupted. And the whirr-

ing of helicopters evacuating the wounded from the front lines
provided a backdrop for the homage being paid to those pilots
who had made their greatest sacrifice.

Both men were recommended for the award of the Congressional Medal of Honor.

CHAPTER 10

TIME FOR DECISION

When the second anniversary of the Korean conflict was marked off the calendars in the bunkers, the truce talks were stalemated.

Army airstrips in Korea outnumbered those of the Air Force six to one, which meant that the light planes could transport passengers and cargo to within jeeping distance of any given unit on the front or anywhere else on the peninsula. Improvements in the construction of these airstrips took on State-side proportions. Hard flooring for the tents, oil heat, makeshift showers, neo-American Standard latrines, electric lights, Quonset huts for operations offices and even radio control towers brightened the real estate. Combat pressures oscillated with the current probing actions. And there was time, much time, for griping and calendar-marking during the era of the "Rotation Reveries".

THE INGENUITY *of the airmen resulted in control towers like the one at the 40th Division strip. Made of the castoff bubble of a wrecked F-51, scrap wood and canvas, the tower was heated for the comfort of the radio operator.*

SOME OF THE OPERATIONS SHACKS *took on Stateside architectural proportions, like this one at I Corps headquarters strip at Uijongbu.*

OTHER OPERATIONS SHACKS *on the front lines, like the IX Corps office near Chunchon, stood out for its art work.*

Names like "Mary", "Helen", "Madge" and "Bonnie" brightened the passenger manifests as USO troupes were transported by Army air. Junketing Congressmen, newly released from probing constituents and the merry-go-round of Washington politics, cascaded into Korea to see for themselves what the "boys" were doing. And they found out by using their ducats on the "pee wee" airlines.

The "brass" flights all began at "Dragon Flight" which was situated at an abandoned horse racetrack on the east side of Seoul. Their runway was the south side of the track several furlongs in length. The racetrack formed an efficiently operated pinwheel which turned out a great volume of daily light plane traffic. Because the place was so busy, it was dubbed the "LaGuardia of Korea". Because of its construction, the racetrack could accommodate simultaneously and without confusion the Army's light aircraft which might be landing, taxiing to take off, taxiing to passenger-drop stations and even taking off. The "LaGuardia of Korea" enjoyed an international reputation among the great of the world's statesmen, military men and civilians who made use of its services. The passenger terminal contained a rack of identification placards having one to five stars for visiting Army, Navy and Air Force generals or admirals. In addition, there were Army and Navy seals for the secretaries of the Army and Navy who might be passing through. The placards were slipped into brackets on the aircraft before takeoff. War correspondents flying to various field units used the detachment's services almost daily.

One of the distinctive features of the racetrack was that it was the only light plane airport in the world which completely surrounded a cabbage farm, the raw ingredients from which is made kimchi, the Korean national food delicacy. Out of consideration for the Korean farmers who were attempting to supplement their scarce food supply, this agricultural enterprise was allowed to continue while the Army operations were in force.

Another distinctive feature of the Racetrack provided a constant source of amusement to Americans and Koreans alike. A trolley line of Toonerville vintage ran parallel to the runway. The trolley's suspension cable once extended the full length of the south side of the strip. Since the wires constituted a menace to navigation in an already difficult landing area, the trolley company obligingly removed the wires for a stretch of about 100 yards. The tracks were left in their original position. But in order to pass the wireless section of its circuit, the trolley had to be run at full speed. Usually it could coast the 100 yards and a fast-moving conductor was able to re-establish contact with the suspension cable. But if a heavy load or an unusually strong headwind braked the car to a halt, the passengers good-naturedly dismounted and pushed the car until contact could be re-established. The airmen of the "Dragon Flight" never did find out if the fares of the passengers were ever exchanged for the pushing.

In spite of the many months during which the light planes operated from the Racetrack, dozens of Korean civilians, young and old, gathered there to watch the unarmed and unarmored "pyangi" take to the air. The drawing cards for the "horsey" set were the airborne steeds on whom no bets were placed for the best in the race, for the "Dragon Flight" stable had a winner in every stall.

On their monotonous "taxi" runs all over the peninsula, the "flyboys" found relief from boredom by maintaining a listening watch on their VHF Army radio channel, 122.5. During the normal day's flying, the listening aviators might hear the voices of flying buddies calling for landing instructions into airstrips miles away. Or they might be entertained by an aspiring Caruso anonymously projecting a questionable tenor into the airwaves of the "Land of the Morning Calm". Or they might even be gripped by the drama of pilots seeking help when caught in foul weather or by mechanical difficulties in flight. Their radio channel became their party line for information, entertainment and education.

THE RACETRACK, *home of the "Dragon Flight" at Seoul.*

The most entertaining transmissions heard by the Army Aviators were illegal. On one occasion, a USO singer being transported in an L-19 was prompted by her mischievous pilot to entertain the listening watch for a full five minutes with renditions of popular songs. The "bravos" echoed all over the front. Little did she realize, however, that her potential audience included Generals Ridgway and Van Fleet who were also in flight at the time. Unfortunately for the Generals, they were not wearing their earphones during the impromptu show. But their pilots enjoyed it, despite their apprehension that someone might be "reamed" for the shenanigans.

The international associations which were experienced by the pilots from the Racetrack had their compensating moments. During the visit of Field Marshal Earl Alexander of Great Britain in June, his personal secretary and four aides were transported to the 1st British Commonwealth Division airstrip in an L-20 by Lt. William G. Phillips of Weatherford, Oklahoma. Their visit completed some time later, the L-20 began its takeoff run from the short strip. But when two-thirds of the strip had passed him by with his wheels still on the ground, Phillips cut his switches and applied his brakes. The Beaver skidded past the end of the runway, sheared its landing gear in a shallow ditch, and came to rest ingloriously in a mine field. As the dust settled in the cabin of the plane, the silence of the distinguished passengers was broken by a timid voice calling from the rearmost seat in a decidedly British accent: "I say, may we get out now?"

The Army Aviators became increasingly public relations conscious as time allowed. One venture in which they embarked to lift the morale among themselves was abetted by Jack Jarvis, the night editor of the Seattle (Washington) Post-Intelligencer. Jarvis amused himself with the hobby of producing wallet-size cards which enrolled unsuspecting victims in such fictitious organizations as "The I've Met a Lot of

I'm An ARMY Flyer
And Proud Of It
ASSOCIATION
("AIR FORCE? WHAT'S THAT?")

MEMBER (Time Indefinite)

VOID IF SIGNED BY JACK JARVIS, SEATTLE,
WHO TURNED OUT THIS CARD FOR 8th ARMY'S FLYERS
"SOMEWHERE IN KOREA"

Admirals and I'm Not Impressed Association", "The Society of Hard Luck Motorists", "The More I See of Humans The Better I Like Dogs Association", "Bottlenecks Unlimited", "Neurotics Unanimous" and "The Everyone Here But Me Is a Son of a Bitch Association". Jarvis contributed identification cards to Army Aviators in Korea so that they could prove their identity without confusion with Air Force pilots.

Another of their gimmicks was a certificate which enrolled distinguished passengers in the "Brotherhood of 38th Parallel Crossers".

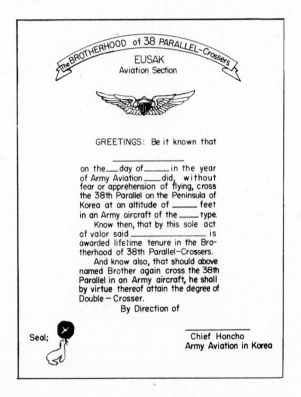

The designation of "Honorary Army Aviator" was conferred upon Lt. Gen. John W. "Iron Mike" O'Daniel in July, just prior to his leaving command of the US I Corps at Uijongbu. "Iron Mike" had proved himself an enthusiastic supporter of the "flyboys" in Korea, as well as in Europe where, on one occasion, he personally reconnoitered the Siegfried Line in advance of his spearheading 3rd Inf. Div. During ceremonies presided over by Lt. Col. J. Elmore Swenson, General O'Daniel was presented with one of the Jarvis identification cards and a set of wings.

```
                    Army Aviators in Korea
                           APO 301

                                             6 July 1952

    SUBJECT:  Designation as Honorary Army Aviator

    TO      :  Lieutenant General John W. O'Daniel

    FROM    :  Chief Army Aviator in Korea

            1.  Designation of Honorary Army Aviator is here-
    with awarded to Lieutenant General John W. O'Daniel by the
    Army Aviators in Korea.

            2.  Basis for award is unwritten regulation which
    permits designation of Honorary Army Aviator to military
    personnel who meet basic flight requirements.

            3.  Lieutenant General O'Daniel, by logging more
    than 500 hours as a passenger in Army aircraft, has won his
    wings as "The Flying General".

            4.  By virtue of his ability to fly as a passenger in
    Army aircraft without fear of pilots' capabilities and without
    apprehension of airsickness, Lieutenant General O'Daniel
    has shown his qualifications to carry the attached card which
    identifies him as an Honorary Army Aviator.

            5.  Designation of Honorary Army Aviator entitles
    Lieutenant General O'Daniel to all privileges accruing to
    Army Aviators in Korea.

                              J. ELMORE SWENSON
                              Lt Col          Arty
                          Chief Army Aviator in Korea
```

The recognition afforded the efforts of the Army Aviators
reached international proportions. In August, the Hwarang
Medal with Silver Star was awarded to Captain Hubert D.
Gaddis, a helicopter pilot attached to the 8063rd MASH. The
presentation was made by Maj. Gen. Kim Chong Ho, commander of the 9th ROK Inf. Div. at ceremonies during the
Korean Liberation Day celebration on 15 August. Gaddis was
cited for meritorious service in evacuating sick and wounded
ROKA soldiers during the June combat operations.

The Tulsa, Oklahoma, pilot had the distinction of being the
only Army Aviator to hold an official world's flying record.
On 21 May 1949, he had established the altitude record of

21, 220 feet for helicopters in a flight at Bridgeport, Connecticut. (This record held until the Fall of 1953.) An Army Aviation veteran since 1943, Gaddis had won the Air Medal with five bronze clusters during service with the 28th Inf. Div. in Europe. He added three more during his Korea service.

Meanwhile, a letter of appreciation was given the same month to the 8193rd Hel. Det. by Lt. Gen. Yu Jae Hung, commander of the II ROK Corps. In the letter to Captain Louis Hamner of Columbus, Georgia, commanding officer of the detachment, General Yu cited the Army pilots for operating "under

Capt. Gaddis at the controls of his helicopter making ready for take off.
(U. S. Army Photo)

adverse conditions and in close proximity to the enemy in order to evacuate gravely wounded personnel of my command. You thereby made possible the prompt medical treatment which did much to alleviate suffering and undoubtedly saved many lives." The Army Aviators included in the citation were Lt. Donald Armstrong of Redwood City, California; Lt. Harry E. Zeigler of Roslyn, Pennsylvania; and Lt. James F. Spaulding of Mesa, Arizona.

In the meantime, while the negotiators dickered fruitlessly at the conference table at Panmunjom, the fighting men warded off the annoying probing actions which were being undertaken by the enemy to prod the lines into more advantageous shapes. Actions at Shanghai Heights, T-Bone Hill, White Horse Mountain, Old Baldy, Pork Chop Hill and Bunker Hill reached none of the major proportions of earlier battles. But they provided interludes of action which kept the war alive on the Korean front, if not on the home front Stateside.

Two airmen of the 25th Inf. Div. experienced a thousand-to-one shot in July. Their L-19 had flown head-on into an artillery shell and they lived to tell about it.

Lt. William M. Bogert of Levelland, Texas, and his observer, Lt. Roy E. Bastine of Portsmouth, Ohio, were cruising at about 8,500 feet above enemy territory on the northeastern front when a sudden jolt threw Bogert from the controls.

> "I figured we'd been hit with flak at first. I lost control of the ship for a few seconds and then we levelled off and stayed in the air for an hour to finish our mission. It was like someone had hit your car with a big brick while you were going 70 miles an hour. But from the cockpit, we couldn't see any damage, so we went on with the mission."

Upon landing their aircraft, they found a half-inch groove cut into the lower half of the right wing strut. The right side of the fuselage was scraped and dented below the cockpit. It was later determined that the markings had been left by an artillery shell which evidently had sideswiped the strut first and then had deflected into the side of the plane.

> "Luckily, the detonator never touched the plane," Bogert said. "If the shell had been half an inch higher or if we had been flying half an inch lower, it would have blown us out of the sky."

And they'll never know if the shell was stamped CCF or USA.

Regardless of the action, or lack of it, on the fighting front, the work of the helicopters was never done. The flood season of 1952 was a case in point. More than 1, 200 marooned UN soldiers were plucked from flood areas where they had been cut off.

Aerial view of MASH, 8063 AU.   (U. S. Army Photo)

The Army choppers helped to evacuate 800 UN troops stranded at a Quartermaster service center southwest of Chunchon in July when flood waters of the Pukhan River created an island out of their position and threatened to cover it. In a four-hour long operation, all but twelve men were evacuated. The remaining dozen remained on the island to guard the material left there.

The Army helicopter pilots also engaged in another mercy operation, this time with civilians isolated by flood waters in the village of Bamsum, west of Seoul. Food, medicines and a doctor were airlifted to the village of 350 natives who had been cut off by the flooded Han River.

Two helicopters of the 8192nd Hel. Det. snatched to safety a total of 89 men trapped by a flash flood while fording a stream of the Soyang River in the northeast sector in August. The men were on a training exercise after the typhoon "Karen" had passed through the area. Captain Robert H. Williams of Denton, Texas, and Lt. Henry H. Tomme of Livingston,

Texas, brought the men to safety after a truck carrying 25 men was washed downstream, a Bailey bridge was washed out by rushing waters, and other soldiers were cut off on an island near the river.

Meanwhile, on the eastern front, 206 men of the 3rd Division were evacuated by five helicopter pilots in a two and one-half hour rescue operation. These men were trapped by flood waters which rose almost 25 feet on 28 July. The stranded American soldiers and Korean Service Corps troops were evacuated one at a time by the helicopters which transported them to dry land a mile away. The rescuing pilots included Captain Norman I. Anderson of Laredo, Texas; Captain Colin D. Ciley, Jr. of Arlington, Virginia; Lt. Robert W. Blakely of Seattle, Washington; Major Charles A. Johnson of Paradise, California; and Captain Erling C. Biorge of Baltimore, Maryland.

On the 2nd Division front, two helicopter pilots evacuated 34 soldiers from a lump of ground so small that its occupants had to dangle over the edges to make room for the choppers to land. Lt. William F. Kummer of Lewiston, Idaho, and Lt. Willard C. Hartley of Hollydale, California, made 17 landings each on the bulldozed mound of dirt as the swirling waters edged closer to a stranded American soldier and his 33 ROKA companions. The pilots described the island as "about the size of a teacup saucer", 22 feet long and 10 feet wide. As they neared the isolated spot on each trip, the remaining "prisoners" crawled down the slope and hung on at the water's edge until the helicopter landed. So tiny was the landing area, Hartley said later, that the aircraft's tail rotor rested in the water on the low side of the mound.

Flood, famine and front line fighting had drawn the best of the small group of men who flew the "Whirlybirds" in Korea. But there were still other missions, less glamorous, perhaps, because they were flown behind the lines, but nevertheless vital to "Operation Grasshopper".

Night evacuations of sick and wounded UN soldiers were performed a number of times in Korea. But the mission of Captain Guy C. Meiss of Nescopeck, Pennsylvania, proved to be novel in several respects. Meiss' usual job was that of executive officer of the Eighth Army Flight Detachment and personal pilot to General Van Fleet. He was called early one morning in September to evacuate a soldier suffering a ruptured appendix at the 3rd Division Replacement Company several miles north of Seoul. Accompanied by Lt. Col. (then

A helicopter bearing a wounded soldier takes off from the medical collection point enroute to a rear echelon hospital, in Korea.
(*U. S. Army Photo*)

Major) Gerald H. Shea of Carmel, California, Meiss was guided by flashlight to a landing in a ball park. After picking up his patient, Meiss felt his way at low altitude through a thick fog rising off the Han River to the 121st Evacuation Hospital at Yongdongpo which was reached as dawn broke. Within minutes, the soldier was undergoing treatment. Meiss, meanwhile, returned to his base and his regularly assigned mission of flying the Army Commander on a tour of the front line units later that same day.

Army Aviators in Korea had long been convinced that there was no such thing as "rear" area flying on that peninsula. Every flight involved contact with a "front" of some kind, whether the enemy, the terrain or the weather.

Captain Sidney Achee of Salinas, California, was serving as administrative officer for the Aviation section at Eighth Army Headquarters in Taegu when he volunteered for a helicopter rescue mission. The call for help came on a day when Army aircraft in many sections of Korea had been grounded because of high winds up to 60 mph and high turbulence in the mountainous areas. The 49th Fighter Group at the Taegu Air Force base asked that an Army helicopter be dispatched to pick up a pilot who had bailed out of his burning F-84 jet somewhere near Taegu. The position of the downed pilot, Lt. Jack Sturm of Phoenix, Arizona, was confused by reports placing him in three different areas within a 30-mile

radius of Taegu. His exact location was relayed to the rescuing Army chopper pilot by the leader of a flight of six Air
Force jets which was in contact with Sturm through the emergency VHF radio set which is part of the escape kit provided
each pilot.

Achee found the wind at altitude of such velocity that his helicopter could make little headway. He had to descend to low
altitude and to fight the turbulence through the valleys. At
one time, he flew under high tension wires between two hills
when his rotary-wing aircraft could not be lifted over them.
As a result of being forced to fly at such low altitudes, navigation was difficult. The jets which had located their downed
wing mate made passes at the helicopter to point out the route
to reach the pick-up area. The blasts from the jets were
"tremendous", Achee said. After flying for an hour on a trip
which would normally take 25 minutes, Achee spotted Sturm
in a deep narrow gorge into which the wind had drifted him.
With the control of the helicopter difficult in the high wind
which tunneled through the gorge, the Army Aviator managed
to land his craft on the brink of a steep cliff. With his mechanic, Corporal Donald P. Bjarkman of San Fernando,
California, who had volunteered to go on the flight, Achee
found Sturm surrounded by 50 Koreans who had been trying
unsuccessfully to fashion a litter from the pilot's parachute
in order to carry out the injured flyer.

Because of the wildness of the terrain, the helicopter could
be brought no closer than 400 yards to the injured man. The
two Army airmen carried a litter to Strum, whom they found
bordering on shock as a result of a painful break in the upper
part of his right leg. With the assistance of the Koreans,
Sturm was carried to the helicopter. The trip over those
400 yards took half an hour. Meanwhile, the jets continued
to circle over the rescuers and the rescued. When the litter
had been placed in its pod on the side of the helicopter, Achee
found that the wind conditions would not permit taking an additional passenger. Bjarkman was sent to a neighboring village to contact the National Police for transportation back to
Taegu. He was picked up later by an Air Force ground party
which had been dispatched to locate the crashed aircraft.
After a thirty-minute flight, Sturm was taken by ambulance to
the 25th Evacuation Hospital for treatment. The entire operation, from the mission's request to completion, had taken
two and one-half hours under dangerous flying conditions.
It had been Sturm's first ride in a helicopter and his first
bail-out in Korea in the short month he had been in the theater. But he was an experienced parachutist, since he was
a veteran of two jumps during World War II.

Achee insisted that his mission was one of many daily occur-
rences in Korea. He spoke with authority after flying 80
combat missions with the 25th Inf. Div. aviation section before undertaking his Taegu assignment. But his fellow airmen said that his feat merely proved once again that there
was no such thing as rear-echelon flying in Korea.

Much to the embarrassment of Army Aviation, it was responsible for training a pilot who, for a very short period of time,
became personal pilot to Nam Il, the North Korean Red czar.

On 3 December 1952, at 1010 hours, L-19 number 51-4794,
flown by 2nd Lt. Kug Yong Am, a student Army Aviator at
the ROKA school, took off from Kwangju and failed to return
to base at the completion of a training flight. An extensive
air search was fruitless. Monitors of Pyongyang Radio reported that the North Koreans had announced with great ju-
bilation that Lt. Kug had deserted to the NKA and had landed
his aircraft on the airfield at Pyongyang mid great ceremony
which included being decorated by Nam Il himself who immediately appointed the ex-ROK officer as his flying aide.

Red-faced ROK and US army officials immediately established that Kug's L-19 had been due for AOCP (aircraft out of
commission for parts), since the right brake was faulty.
They also found that Kug was a North Korean whose mother
lived in Pyongyang. Apparently, Kug had been contacted by
a Red agent with whom plans had been made far in advance
for the "bug-out". There were many North Korean officers
serving in the ROK army. All of them had been found faithful in the conduct of their duties. But as a result of the Kug
affair, all ROK Army Aviators in training at Kwangju were
re-screened. Eleven of those who were found to have rela-
tives in North Korea were released from further training
to preclude any further incidents.

Kug's tenure as a "hero" was short-lived. Within three weeks
of his flight to the north, the underground reported he had
been assassinated. And Nam Il had never found out what it
was like to fly in an American-made light Army aircraft.

More damaging than the loss of aircraft and pilot was the
excitement caused among some UN troops who reported enemy light aircraft operations over the front. None of these
reports were substantiated. But on 22 December, anti-
aircraft batteries of the 3rd Division fired on one of its own
Army aircraft. Fortunately, the L-19 was not hit.

Control Tower and headquarters quonset of the 7th Infantry Division.

CHAPTER 11

THE CALM
BEFORE THE PEACE

As the third Christmas in Korea for the UN troops approached, the high hopes for peace which had reached a climax during the early months of 1952 simmered out of the hopes of Army Aviators. Their existence became one of watchful waiting. Uppermost in their thoughts were those of home.

In the meanwhile, history was repeating itself for the Signal Corps. Back in World War I days, that branch of the service was the first to undertake the infant air arm as a part of its activity. After a lapse of several decades, the Signal Corps again had taken to the airways to perform its important mission of maintaining the Army communications chan-

1st Lt. Marion R. Marker of Canton, Ohio; Capt. Walter G. Pitt of Duluth, Minnesota; and PFC Jack M. Carter of Merced, California, unload mail for troops in the central front at U. S. X Corps Airstrip.
(U. S. Army Photo)

nels. The 304th Signal Operations Battalion in Seoul had established a five-man aviation section in 1951. Their primary mission was to deliver official mail throughout Korea. During the first year of their operations, this small unit had delivered 311,965 pounds of mail. Single loads of as much as 450 pounds had been carried. Through the efforts of this small group of men, one of the many problems of the Army in Korea was solved: that of commander communicating with commander.

At the same time, an important change in Army Aviation maintenance operations was made when the Ordnance Corps was relieved of its responsibilities. Ordnance had served as an indifferent middleman between Army commands and the Air Force, which actually procured aircraft for the Army. Onto the scene came the Transportation Corps, born of World War II necessity, whose short history had closely paralleled that of Army Aviation in its meteoric rise as an important part of the Army team. To them, therefore, went the future responsibility of procurement and maintenance of Army aircraft, both fixed and rotary-wing. They undertook their new mission with an enthusiasm which had been conspicuous by its absence during the tenure of the Ordnance Corps. The OLAM's now became the TAAMCO's (Transportation Corps Army Aviation Maintenance Companies).

During the first week of September 1952, the first award of the Meritorious Unit Commendation to an Army Aviation section was made to the "Dragon Flight". The Detachment was cited for the period 22 March 1951 to 1 August 1952 for performance of duties, for tireless effort, for its high degree of technical skill and its outstanding safety record under extremely adverse and hazardous conditions. The citation also recorded that:

> "Although the mission assigned to the members of the detachment was primarily administrative, they were often called upon to accomplish liaison with units operating in extreme forward areas which were normally considered to be inaccessible to the low-performance aircraft assigned to their unit."

Then, Hollywood came to Korea for the filming by Columbia Pictures Corporation of the first commercial motion picture ever made concerning Army Aviation. "Mission Over Korea" was to tell the story of Army Aviation operations during the early days of the Korean conflict when fabric-covered L-5's were used to seek out the enemy and to bring friendly artillery fire upon them. The story revolved around the operations of a field artillery battalion's aviation section consisting of two pilots and three crewmen. Action in the picture began on Kyushu, Japan, where the first scenes of the film were taken by the Columbia crew consisting of Producer Robert Cohn, Director Fred Sears, Director of Photography Bill Whitley, Cameraman Emil Oster and Grip (equipment handler) Frank Mitchell. The Department of the Army assigned Lt. Dario Politella of Kent, Ohio, to act as technical advisor to the Hollywood men. The Army Aviators who did the flying for the picture in the Far East were Lt. Marvin Siddle of Danville, Virginia; Lt. Donald Cheney of Waco, Texas; and Lt. Ernest R. Taft of Rochester, Illinois. "Mission Over Korea" had the added distinction of being the first commercial motion picture to be filmed extensively in the combat theater.

The five-man camera team arrived in Tokyo on 14 September and flew immediately with its 2,800 pounds of camera equipment to Itazuke AFB in the south where for ten days of excellent weather, the preliminary sequences of the film were ground out. Then an over-water flight to Korea in a C-47 and three L-5 aircraft was made to complete the film at six locations: Inchon, Kwangju firing point #9, Suhbong-ri, Pia-ri, Taegu and Uijongbu. At the end of every day's shooting, the film was carefully wrapped and shipped by air to Hollywood via Tokyo. Since none of the stars who were later dubbed into the picture had come to Korea, Siddle, Cheney and Politella acted as stand-ins for them. The picture was completed on 27 October. During the shooting schedule, Army Aviation provided the crew with transportation in every type aircraft available in Korea. Columbia paid the shot at the going hourly rate. A total of 75:40 hours was put on the L-5's, 37:40 hours on the L-20 that was used to carry cargo and personnel, and 16 hours on the H-13 which was used as a camera platform at all locations. The L-17 was used for a one-hour flight. Cost of this flying time came to slightly under $3,000.

Probably the most interesting flying project undertaken for the film was the firing of a bazooka which was mounted under the right wing of Cheney's L-5. The rig was devised by OLAM at Ascom City and the firing was done at Pia-ri just north of Kwangju. A second L-5 piloted by Siddle carrying the camera and Camerman Emil Oster, filmed the firing of the rocket from close formation.

The motion picture was released for public showing in August 1953.

The newest service to join the Army Aviation team was the Medical Service Corps which provided seven officers to take the Helicopter Transport Pilots course at Fort Sill, Oklahoma, on 6 October. The 22-week course would qualify them to fly with MASH units exclusively.

Death struck at the Army Aviators again during the Fall. On 2 November, a 7th Division L-19 piloted by Lt. Clyde P. Johnson was hit by ack-ack fire. His observer, Lt. Walter W. Winkler of Champaign, Illinois, was killed, but Johnson was able to parachute to safety even though he had been wounded in the leg and his parachute had been riddled by shell fragments. Johnson had tried to push Winkler out of the plane, but the observer was already dead. A short time later, the two airmen who had replaced this pair were accidentally hit by friendly v.t. artillery of the neighboring 3rd Division. The L-19 was piloted by Lt. Sam Dugan when it was hit over the Alligator Jaws. He and his observer, Lt. Rosensweig, bailed out. Dugan was not seriously injured, but his observer suffered 2nd and 3rd degree burns which hospitalized him in Japan for several months.

Meanwhile, the presidential elections of 1952 found a new interest for the airmen. One of the Republican campaign promises was that a speedy end to the Korean conflict would be found. Candidate Dwight D. Eisenhower pledged a first-hand look at the war. When the General was elected, the Army Aviators looked forward to a fulfillment of this promise to visit Korea, since it would fall upon them to transport the President-elect on any tour of the fighting front he might make. "Ike" became, by far, the most distinguished passenger ever to be flown by the "pee-wee" airlines in Korea. Extraordinary security measures were taken during his visit, and everywhere the President-elect was flown in the light Army planes, a cover of Air Force fighter aircraft circled the slow-flying L-19's.

The President-elect had been one of Army Aviation's strongest proponents in Europe during World War II. "Ike" had learned to fly Cubs in 1939 when he was stationed in the Philippines. In 1941, during the Louisiana maneuvers, he had piloted an Army light plane while inspecting units in the field. A civilian aviation executive who was with him at the time later wrote:

"After we took off from a narrow little machine gun range, I turned the controls over to him and he flew for the rest of the day, flying 12 miles to inspect a bivouac area from the air, then 22 miles in another direction to check on something else. It was difficult navigation, but he was remarkably accurate. I was quite impressed because he hadn't flown for several years, and the field on which he made his final landing was anything but desirable. "

During World War II, the President, at that time commanding the troops which were engaged in the "Crusade in Europe" used the Piper Cubs for inspection tours of the front. One of the few pictures ever taken of Eisenhower at the controls of an aircraft was taken in an Army L-4.

When Ike arrived in Korea, he was prepared for the quick inspection tour which a greatly expanded Army Aviation provided for him.

Lt. Col. J. Elmore Swenson, the Aviation Officer at EUSAK, assigned himself the mission of acting as the General's personal pilot. He explained this by saying:

"Because I was in charge of all Army Aviation in Korea, the responsibility for the safety of the President was mine, regardless of whether I sat in my office in Eighth Army headquarters or whether I was actually doing the flying. So I elected to fly the General personally. "

Colonel Swenson described his mission more fully.

"Flying in light planes in a combat theater was old stuff to the General, who was an old Cub pilot himself as well as a passenger on many occasions in Europe during World War II when he served as commander of SHAEF. Ike reminded me of his familiarity with the light Army planes on the first flight out of Dragon Base at Seoul.

" 'I used to fly planes of this type, ' he said.

"The President was wrapped up in a fur parka due to the five degrees below zero cold. With the help of my crew chief, Sgt. Tom D. Burnaugh of Burbank, California, we buckled him into the L-19 with the safety belt and shoulder harness. The President commented that the safety harness 'must be a new gadget', and I explained to him that it was the best safety feature on the plane. But I didn't dare mention it was a crash safety feature, since I did not want him to be apprehensive about the flight over the rugged terrain. This was part of my effort to make him at ease. I also made sure that during his two days of flying with us there would be no violent turns, that landing approaches would be long and gradual, and that all landings would be 'greased' on all three points.

"Even though I was sure that the President did not need to be sold on Army Aviation operations, this flight would prove an opportunity for grass-roots public relations which we could not afford to miss.

"On the first day's flying itinerary was the 1st US Marine Division airstrip which was located northeast of the peace camp at Munsan-ni. On this occasion, as on every other flight of Army aircraft carrying the President and his party, F-51 fighter aircraft provided cover. En route to the Marine installation, I pointed out the balloons hovering over the truce camp at Panmunjom, the eagle-shaped peace camp at Munsan-ni, and the Han River. Ike was noncommittal during the flight. But when we made a long landing approach through the hills, the General said: 'We sure came down through those hills fast.'

"After we landed, he had a little trouble unlocking his safety belt. 'I'm getting too damn fat,' he said by way of explanation.

"Everywhere the President went he was surrounded by newsmen who hung on his every word. Photographers representing the world press clicked their shutters innumerable times to record his every move in Korea. But I felt that I was in an enviable position, since there is something about two men alone in a flimsy aircraft which develops an intimacy no newsman can achieve in doing his job. As a result, I believe I was able to get a better reaction of the General's visit to Korea than has ever been reported in the press. Many times during the inspection trip, as we sat in the L-19 waiting for takeoff, I looked out at the reporters and photographers staring at us behind the plexiglass windows and thought: 'What they wouldn't give to be sitting in my place, alone with the most important man in the world.'

"On one occasion, during a breather between flights, the General was talking about his rise to the Presidency and the Korean situation. 'You know,' he said, 'I never wanted to get into this political mess, but since I am in it, I'll give it everything I've got. '

"The racetrack airstrip at Seoul became our base of operations for flying the President. The pilots of Dragon Flight were assigned the task of flying the presidential party consisting of Secretary of Defense Charles E. Wilson, Attorney General Herbert Brownell, General Omar Bradley, General Mark W. Clark, General James A. Van Fleet, and a secret service agent. The Dragon Flight pilots were some of the best in Korea, hand-picked for the mission of flying VIP's in Korea. Extraordinary precautions were taken to insure the safety of the distinguished passengers. Each was flown in a separate aircraft, because if all were bundled into a single plane, any accident might result in a multiple tragedy. Air Force fighter cover protected them against any stray enemy aircraft which might penetrate southward. And the itinerary was kept top secret even from the pilots until the moment of takeoff.

"On the second day of the presidential 'rat race', we took off from the Racetrack at 0800 hours through a thick, smoky haze which was common around Seoul at that time of year. The field was socked in with a quarter-mile of visibility. But we broke out of the haze at 800 feet. The General was more relaxed on this trip and more talkative than he had been the first day.

"During our flight from the ROK Capitol Division, General Van Fleet asked me to fly to 2,000 feet and circle twice north of Chorwon so that the President could see the front. One of our air strikes had been going on just before we took off, but it was calm and peaceful except for a column of black smoke rising in the air from the enemy lines. I pointed out Chorwon, White Horse Mountain and the Iron Triangle. He took a long look out there, especially at White Horse Mountain. All I could think of was: 'If the Chinese only knew that their lines were being watched by the next President of the United States. '

"On our way back to Seoul I explained a little of the ROK Army Aviation training program and the General opened up a little. 'Their potential is terrific and they are very intent, ' he said. 'They even seem to take their training more intently than our own GI's. They are very intent and eager to learn. '

"When we landed at our airstrip at Seoul, the ground crewmen came over with their cameras and the General said: 'I guess these are all the amateurs. We've been posing for the professionals all day. '

"The men got their photos. And my job was done. "

The Christmas season also brought other notables to be flown across Korea. These included Cardinal Spellman, who spent his second Christmas with the troops, and Evangelist Billy Graham.

The lull in the fighting at this time was pointed up one day at a briefing of staff officers at EUSAK when the briefing officer reported that during a 24-hour period, only four mortar shells had fallen on the entire front.

It was during this period of late 1952 also that the first helicopter fatality of the entire war was recorded when Captain Ralph Brown of the 47th TAAMCO hit a power line near Seoul while on a routine flight.

The new year found Army Aviation forging ahead. A new aircraft was delivered for use by the Eighth Army Commander and his staff. The L-23 was a multi-place, twin-engine

This plane is used for command purposes by the U. S. Army.
(U. S. Army Photo)

Beech Bonanza which was well-suited for transporting high-ranking "brass" with speed and comfort. Of course, its operations were limited to airstrips with open approaches and long runways, but its appearance marked a new era for the "puddle-jumpers". This was the first time that Army Aviation had made a bid for the multi-engine field.

The first L-23 had been dispatched by the Army to Korea on 30 September 1952. The plane was placed in charge of Captain James Lefler, loaded on a Navy flattop and transported to Japan. The plane arrived in Korea on 1 December after flying across the Sea of Japan. The plane worked out so well for the purpose for which it was intended that the "rat race" flying of earlier days died out. Senior officers who used the L-23 reported their pleasure with the rapid transportation offered, as well as for the comfort provided. And at last Army Aviation had a "safe" aircraft for the use of general officers, many of whom in the past had expressed some concern for flying in single engine aircraft.

New developments in the States found the Air Training Department at Fort Sill being graduated into the Army Aviation School as authorized by Army General Order #9, dated 16 January 1953. This step was significant because it was now obvious that Army Aviation was being recognized at last as a function of primary importance to the Army. The Army order creating the School as a Class I installation paved the way for Army Aviation to shed itself of the outside interference it had experienced for more than ten years. Army Aviation was coming into its own.

Meanwhile, the pioneer work in night flying which was laid by Major Hoffman of the 2nd Division in April 1951 was resumed in 1953. Major James Hill of the 7th Inf. Div. aviation section conducted some experiments with little success. Major William Edler of I Corps Artillery experienced a greater degree of success in working with radar fixes of the aircraft which were used to mark targets for the fire control centers on the ground. But his experiments proved that this method was not very accurate. Another pioneer was Major John W. Givens of IX Corps Artillery who sent his ROKA pilots out on pre-dawn missions in the central sector.

But the greatest success with "round-the-clock" observation was achieved by Major Raymond R. Evers of Rantoul, Illinois, the aviation officer of the 7th Division. Upon his arrival at the Division aviation section on 1 February, Evers found a group of pilots who had been experimenting since 25

January with night operations in that rugged terrain. Evers had previously served with the 40th Division aviation section and later as executive officer of the aviation section, EUSAK. The 7th Division airstrip at this time was located at Chipori. The strip was fairly open, with a hill on the south end. Spark-plugging the night operations was Captain Melville Rorick of Colorado, who was termed by Evers to be "one of the most eager and one of the best pilots in the business". Evers planned his operation in advance. Request was made of Eighth Army that a full strength of pilots be assigned so that five pilots would be detailed to night duty without causing undue strain on the day crew. Cooperation was forthcoming from Colonel Swenson, insofar as the availability of pilots allowed. The blessing of Maj. Gen. Wayne Smith, the Division commander, was easy to get, since he was convinced that night flying could be successful. The experiment proved his faith, although this faith had been colored by helicopter flights the General had made in the rear areas at high altitudes.

Here is Major Evers' story of the experiment.

"We planned the operation so as to eliminate all possible hazards because we realized that one accident would brand us a bunch of grandstanders. We picked our best aircraft for night flights. We would not permit flights normally unless the ceiling was at least 2,000 feet above the 4,000-foot hills in the target area. We kept our base radio set in operation at all times to relay weather information, which was vital at that time of year, since it seemed that the weather moved from south to north. All night-flying aircraft were equipped with bomb shackles for flares. All pilots picked for the night missions were instrument-qualified insofar as possible, and all of the pilots and observers were volunteers. Since we were unable to get a field lighting set immediately, we began operations with flare pots fashioned from #10 cans filled with sand soaked with gasoline.

"We established close liaison with the Air Force radar units. Each pilot on his first few flights had these people bring him home just for practice and to build up his confidence in the radar capabilities. I felt that this practice was essential to aggressive operation which was highly desirable if the experiment was to prove successful. Each pilot was also instructed on the procedure for contacting two Air Force bases in the area for GCA (ground control approach) if the weather trapped him to the north. We started the round-the-clock observations about 15 February with a no-moon condition on a black night. The snow was still on the north sides of the hills and even with starlight alone, the pattern of the ridge lines made orientation fairly accurate for the pilots.

"My own first flight was a revelation. I had presumed that we were fighting an ox-cart enemy. It wasn't so. There were vehicles 'out the kazoo' and no oxen in sight. One of our first projects was to determine the routes of enemy supply and his supply dump areas. This was not a difficult situation to handle, since on those black nights the enemy had to travel with their lights on all the way down to the turn-around area. Most of these areas were out of artillery range, but one night after about a week's operation, one air crew finally managed to find an enemy unloading area within 155-gun range. By this time the moon was between the first quarter and half full. Three trucks in the area were brought under fire. One burned, another was hit, and a near-miss resulted on the third, so that the full extent of the damage could not be determined. The pilot turned back without adjusting any more artillery. The first thing I wanted to know was why the devil they left the target without finishing the job. Here is the story. During the afternoon of the same day, their L-19 had been used for briefing an infantry patrol leader on a night mission assigned to him for that night. He had been sick in the aircraft, but it had been cleaned out upon its return to base. You are familiar with L-19 heaters - they had not been cleaned. That evening, about the time the observer had started his adjustment, he became ill from the fumes and tossed his cookies. The pilot took up the adjustment. But even with the windows open he began getting sick from the stench, got vertigo, and had to give up the mission and go home. These are the horrors of our war.

"During the first week of our night operations, one crew knocked out a bridge across the Imjin River which we hadn't been able to get to during the daytime missions because of enemy ack-ack concentrations in the area. Again, the night of this successful mission offered no moon, no artificial lighting - just starlight against the ice. We were most effective in harassing highway traffic on dark nights when they could not drive without lights. As soon as they heard an aircraft, the Reds would stop and turn off their lights. They were out of range, but we could still harass their movement of supplies just by appearing on the scene. We have counted as many as 20 or more vehicles bumper-to-bumper by the light of our parachute flares.

"We knew the targets were there, and the sound of our engines kept them from moving, but if only we had some way of getting fire on them! We worked on the Air Force liaison personnel in the Division to make available divert missions of night-intruding B-26 aircraft. But we had no success. Their answer was that there were more lucrative targets to the north. Of course, we were not particularly impressed with this answer, since we were primarily concerned with the artillery and mortar shells these Reds were bringing down to be rained on the 7th Division troops the next day. So frustrating did this situation become that when I walked out to the flight line one night, I found Rorick attaching 100-pound fragmentation bombs to the wing shackles of his L-19. I still don't know how he got them, but I figured our job was big enough in merely providing observation without taking on tactical bombardment. So I ordered him to pull them off. As I thought about it later, I often wished I had let him go ahead.

"Our experience in night observation showed us that when battlefield illumination was needed quickly in an area not within searchlight capabilities, the illumination could be provided most quickly and accurately by Army aircraft dropping flares. Even though an Air Force C-47 'Gooney Bird' was on call at all times over the front to supply flares, the Air Force pilots could not be as intimately familiar with our area as our own pilots. And where they might have to travel as much as 50 miles to answer our request for flares, we never had to go more than five miles. With an aircraft over the area, we could provide illumination on call within two to two and one-half minutes on any point and, barring excessive winds, the flare would hit the ground within 100 yards of the point designated. This pin-pointing was most important, because a flare dropped in the wrong place might silhouette friendly troops instead of the enemy. Since the effective illumination diameter of a single flare was more than 1,000 yards, our type operation was highly effective. Each L-19 carried four flares, or ten minutes of illumination. These were rigged for release electrically from the shackles under each wing. It would be possible to double this load very easily with the installation of extra shackles, extra switches and wiring. In addition to the aircraft in the air, a second L-19 and crew was kept on the alert on the ground in case of need to provide continuous illumination of the battlefield. Our supply of flares was limited, unfortunately, since our own supply channels were inefficient on this score. But we were able to 'scrounge' a Beaver-load of them from a contact at the Air Force base at Yongdongpo.

"Our experiment with night flying resulted in increased efficiency among our pilots, as well as effective operations against the enemy. One illustration is Rorick's flight of 27 February. During the night, the Division had launched an attack on T-Bone Hill. The ceiling was about 2,000 feet (mean sea level), so we were on the ground when the infantry started yelling for light. Up to this time, the moon notwithstanding, we had received no serious attention from enemy fire at night. But during this mission, Rorick was surprised to find enemy fire coming uncomfortably close to him. His first flares had been dropped just as requested and he had remained in the area to drop his full load in spite of the firing. He was flying at 6-8,000 feet above the terrain. We found out how the enemy had been able to spot him when he circled the field upon his return from the mission. His L-19 was outlined almost as clearly as day against the light overcast.

"I might add here that one of the strongest encouragements for our night flyers was the inaccuracy of enemy countermeasures. They had one hilltop out in front of Old Baldy that would blossom out occasionally at night with 37 millimeter fire, but you always knew that if they hit you at night, it was an accident. "

For his leadership in the night flying experiment, Evers was awarded a cluster to his Bronze Star Medal.

On 11 February 1953, after almost two years in Korea, General James A. Van Fleet left for the States and retirement. One of the last statements he made was a tribute to Army Aviation which, he said, was his "right hand" in Korea, not only because of its value as an effective observation medium, but also as efficient transportation for the Army commanders in that difficult terrain.

Lt. Gen. Maxwell D. Taylor assumed command of Eighth Army. Colonel Swenson pointed out to the new commander that the reason why Army Aviation could operate so well with limited numbers of aircraft and pilots in Korea was because of the centralized operations which had been accomplished in the divisions by the aviation officers. By January 1953, all of the divisions in Korea, excepting the 25th Inf. Div., had combined their infantry and artillery aviation sections for centralized operations. The success of this type operation resulted in experimentation with an Army Aviation Company in the 7th Division in May which had the approval of the new EUSAK commander. By July, all the divisions were experimenting with the AA Company idea when General Taylor indicated to his commanders that Korea provided the time and place to try out the radical idea. The Army Commander also said that neither he nor his subordinate commanders would operate without Army Aviation because it provided the necessary mobility to assure efficient operations for unit commanders.

To add to the versatility of the light plane at war, a plan was concocted by the airmen of the 7th Division whereby the L-19 could be used as a flying rat trap. The idea was not new, since fully a year before a "crackpot" idea of the same type had been germinated in the 3rd Inf. Div. among staff officers who were never able to give it birth. At the time, the story of using the L-19 as a flying rat trap was pooh-poohed throughout Army Aviation circles in Korea. But it took the last months of the war and an Army Aviator named Rorick to give it a whirl. Of Rorick, Major Evers has said:

> "I am firmly convinced that any history of Army Aviation in Korea would be incomplete without a mention of Rorick. That lad had more guts, imagination, drive, love of flying and less respect for any shirker than any officer I knew in Korea. His only flaw was impetuousness. When a suggestion was made of a new project, you never heard: 'It can't be done.' It was always: 'I believe that the best way to do the job is like this.' And he was always ready to do it the first time himself."

General Smith, the Division commander, was anxious to have prisoners which the Seventh had been unable to capture in some weeks. So Rorick decided to embellish the old idea of the 3rd Division and try to get the wily Reds out of their foxholes and bunkers into the open so that the Infantry could capture a few for interrogation. The "bait" he planned to use was "George", a dummy he would parachute out of his L-19 right in front of them. Meanwhile, an ambush patrol would

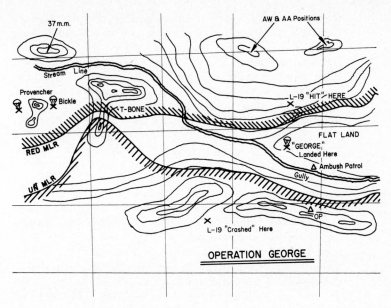

be ready to take prisoner the enemy who would most certainly rush out to capture the dummy.

The stage was set on about 16 February at a stream junction about 2.000 yards east of T-Bone Hill and in no-man's land. Major Evers recounted the mission in detail.

"A number of days were spent in preparation. Rorick practiced several parachute drops with the dummy until he could drop him on a pin point. We coordinated with Division staff so that on the appointed day, before dawn, an infantry patrol was sent out to the gully close to where 'George' was supposed to land. The GI's had to stay out there all day, since the ruse was planned for dusk. The wind came up and it got cold. What a miserable time they must have had. By mid-afternoon, the wind was hitting 25 knots and we were getting calls every 15 minutes from the CP to ask if we were planning to go on with the show. Since the ambush patrol had stayed out in the miserable cold all day and we didn't want to disappoint them, we decided to go ahead with the plan even though the high winds would make pin-pointing the drop of the dummy highly improbable. We hoped the wind would lay a little at dusk, as it usually did.

"To make our mission of dropping the dummy as believable as possible, the plan was to make believe that

Rorick's plane would be hit by enemy fire and 'crash' behind our lines. In order to get the plane over a friendly hill for the simulated crash, we had to drop the dummy from about 2,000 feet where the wind would have been blowing harder than at surface. Luckily, the wind velocity lowered to about 20 knots at sundown. We had a smoke grenade taped to each landing gear strut of the L-19. The door had been removed to make 'George' easier to handle. He weighed a good 140 pounds with his sand-filled, shell-container legs. Rorick flew over the area for about a half hour making like he was on a reconnaissance mission. Then, as the light began to fade he dropped down, pretending to take a closer look at the terrain. He drew the enemy fire he expected as he reached a 2,000-foot altitude. He pulled his throttle all the way back and the L-19 sounded as if it were blowing the exhaust stacks off with the spitting and sputtering which resulted. He yanked the pins from the smoke grenades. Fire flew and smoke swirled as 'George' went over the side. The act was designed to portray a frantic Army Aviator leaving a stricken ship. A few seconds later, the plane 'crashed' behind a hill just barely south of friendly lines. As Rorick headed for home right on the deck, black smoke rolled from behind the hill where we had ignited used engine oil to give the impression that the L-19 had crashed and burned.

"It was an excellent performance, and Joe Chink rushed to the bait. But the dummy which we had hoped to land within 100 yards of the ambush patrol had actually landed about 300 yards away because of the high wind. We were lucky to hit the area at all. But this development forced our patrol to move rapidly westward along the protection of the gulley so as not to expose itself to the enemy who had clambered out of their holes to get at the 'parachutist' almost as soon as it hit the ground. From the enthusiasm of their attack, I guess they needed prisoners almost as badly as we did. The S-3 of the Infantry battalion from which the ambush patrol had been made up was with me in a foxhole several hundred yards away. Seeing that the Chinks might reach the dummy before the trap had been reset, he called down an artillery barrage to slow them down. Slow them down? Brother, it was beautiful. The shells landed in a solid line on the approaching enemy. The few who survived apparently decided that one flyboy wasn't worth it and they took off for home.

Our patrol stayed put until midnight, freezing their tails, but no one came to capture 'George". "

But Rorick's "crackpot" idea would have worked, his fellow airmen still insist, had it not been for the overcautious S-3 and the unexpected accuracy of friendly artillery.

The parachuting activities of the Seventh air section seemed fated during this period. Three days after the "George" affair, Lt. Conrad J. Provencher of Lawrence, Massachusetts, and his observer, PFC Bickle, were shot down within 3,000 yards of the site of the dummy deal. Both men were able to parachute out of their aircraft which had been hit near T-Bone Hill. The two airmen landed about 800 yards apart, with Provencher landing farther away from "George's" resting place than his observer. Provencher was captured almost immediately. But Bickle may have been suspected by the Chinese as the subject of another ruse because he was unmolested for 20 minutes - long enough to be rescued by Lt. Ralph Nielsen, who made a running landing into no-man's land with his helicopter. Meanwhile, Captain Jack Burford searched for Provencher for almost an hour until darkness forced him to abandon his mission. He scoured the area from the friendly lines to a mile inside the enemy lines, flying from ten feet to a hundred feet above the ground. He "chogied" along at 60 miles per hour under constant enemy fire. But Burford was unsuccessful in his search, although he was able to get home without a scratch. A few hours later he discovered that his dangerous flight could not have been successful, since friendly infantry observers had seen the enemy take Provencher prisoner almost as soon as he hit the ground. Both Nielsen and Burford were recommended for the Silver Star for their rescue operations.

And for his activity in the night flying operations of the Seventh, Captain Melvin Rorick was recommended for the Distinguished-Flying Cross.

During the month of March, three Army aircraft were shot down in enemy territory. The first pilot parachuted into enemy hands and was later reported to have died of internal injuries. The second Army Aviator attempted to bail out of his L-19, but his parachute became fouled by his stricken aircraft and he was reported killed. The third flyer rode the plane to his death.

Also during this fateful month, a helicopter pilot flew to the rescue of a GI in the Imjin River where he had been washed by a flash flood. As the helicopter hovered over the water, the GI became excited and grabbed the outer edge of the helicopter's litter rack. This so disturbed the center of gravity of the aircraft that the pilot lost control. The helicopter fell into the river, but both the pilot and the GI were rescued by a second helicopter dispatched to the scene.

On 26 March, west of Pyongyang near the "Square Lake" where Major Larry Loos is suspected to have disappeared, Lt. Landon Reid also of IX Corps Artillery and McAllen, Texas, was shot down when the tail section of his L-19 was hit by enemy anti-aircraft fire. Both Reid and his observer bailed out, even though both were wounded. The Army airmen had been circling a target in preparation for firing. The observer was killed either as a result of his wounds or because his chute failed to open because it had been damaged by shell fragments. Reid was taken prisoner and repatriated during "Big Switch".

And in June 1953, Lt. James D. Labor of the 7th Inf. Div., and his observer, Lt. Linn, were shot down in flames to the west of Old Baldy over enemy territory. The L-19 was hit at an altitude of less than 3,000 feet. Labor was temporarily blinded by fire which broke out in the aircraft, but he was able to parachute into enemy territory. Lt. Linn was killed. Although he was severely burned about the face and hands, Labor was able to walk through three miles of enemy territory back into friendly trenches. After several months in a hospital in Japan, the Army Aviator was returned to Korea to complete his tour of duty.

This was the calm before the peace.

CHAPTER 12

U.S.ARMY
14835

LONGO

LOOKING BACK

The third anniversary of the Korean war found the UN forces there close to peace. For more than a year, Army staff airmen had been making plans for their role in the exchanges of prisoners of war, when and if they would be made.

The pay-off came on 20 April 1953 when Operation Little Switch began. Army Aviation was ready for the vital part which it was to play in transporting the sick and wounded UN POW's who were exchanged during the days following. All of Army Aviation in Korea was joined in this operation, however indirect their efforts may have been. They transported military and civilian observers to Freedom Village and the peace camp at Munsan-ni. They flew correspondents of the world press. They evacuated 683 patients during a six-day operation.

A wounded man is placed aboard an H-19 helicopter for evacuation to a hospital. The use of helicopters for evacuating wounded has cut hours off the time of arrival at hospitals.   (U. S. Army Photo)

The starring role of "Little Switch" went to a newcomer to Korea, the 6th Transportation Helicopter Company, whose advance party had appeared on 16 December 1952. The unit had been formed in the States and comprised six officers, 27 warrant officer pilots, a warrant officer in charge of maintenance and one in charge of administration. These warrant officer pilots were something new to the organization of Army Aviation. Heretofore, all pilot personnel of Army Aviation must have met the prerequisite of being commissioned officers in one of the branches of the Army which were authorized aircraft. During the winter of 1951, however, the Army had accepted for training as helicopter pilots a selected group of enlisted men who were given warrants upon completion of flight training in April 1952. These men were trained for assignment to helicopter transportation companies. The Army felt that it was not necessary for them to be well-rounded in their military backgrounds, since they would not require skills other than those of pilots.

The 6th THC was formed at Fort Bragg, North Carolina, where the unit trained for its mission in Korea. Its arrival at Inchon on 5 February 1953 began a period of testing to justify its existence as an integral part of the Army. The Sixth became the first cargo helicopter unit to be activated by the Army, and the first unit of its type to be used by the Army in a combat theater. The unit was based near Chunchon where an elaborate heliport necessary for its operations was constructed during the months of January and February. On 11 February, a group of pilots departed for Kisarazu Air Force Base in Japan to ferry the first increment of five H-19 helicopters over water to Korea. On 23 February, the first ships arrived. By 24 March, the entire complement of 21 helicopters had been ferried across the 125-mile stretch of the Sea of Japan to Pusan. Their mission made history, for the Sixth was the first helicopter unit to make an extended over-water flight.

On 20 March, even before the last of the helicopters had arrived from Japan, the Sixth received its baptism of fire in Korea. A hurried call from EUSAK sent ten H-19's flying on an emergency resupply mission to forward elements of the 3rd Inf. Div. which had been cut off from normal supply channels by local flood conditions in the "Jackson Heights" area. The mission involved the airlifting of 34,000 pounds of rations, fuel and ammunition to an entire regiment and supporting fire units dispersed along the battle line. Within 80 minutes after the first helicopter had arrived at the base loading point, 30 round trips had been made over a distance of 140 miles. Throughout the mission, the helicopters hauled supplies to within 300 yards of the MLR. On the last trip to the front, enemy mortar rounds fell at one unloading point and inflicted minor damage to one chopper. In spite of the record time already made by the Sixth on this one mission, Transportation Corps officials later said that the same mission with the same number of aircraft would have been accomplished in half the time if the receiving troops had been skilled in the unloading of the cargo helicopters.

Before the arrival of the H-19 in Korea, the H-13 had been used to great advantage by the Army. From the outset, the principle mission of the H-13 had been the evacuation of wounded from front-line positions. In spite of the fact that the H-13 was limited to carrying only two litter patients, an impressive record had been tallied by the small numbers which had been operating with the mobile army surgical hospitals scattered across the front. The arrival of the H-19's boosted the monthly totals of wounded evacuated by air.

On 24 March, Eighth Army headquarters called upon the Sixth for their first large-scale medical evacuation mission in Korea. A flare-up in the fighting near "Old Baldy" had resulted in numerous casualties which required immediate evacuation. Five H-19's were flown directly to the forward regimental clearing stations of the 7th Inf. Div. to pick up the wounded. The chopper loads of four litter patients each were delivered to the 121st Evacuation Hospital at Yongdong-po, a distance of 50 miles. At the end of a four-hour period, 52 patients had been carried to the rear area medical installation for specialized medical treatment. The five choppers had averaged 13 round trips covering a distance of well over 1,300 miles.

The advantages of the H-19 over the old H-13 became obvious. The new helicopter could carry four to six litter cases on a single flight, travel faster, and travel farther. Within the next six months, the Sixth evacuated more than 1,000 casualties to rear area hospitals which were beyond the range of the front-line H-13's.

As was the case with all new equipment which reached Korea, the H-19 Sikorsky and its capabilities were demonstrated to ground commanders. These demonstrations were held during the first two weeks of April and they unknowingly provided the prelude to the biggest demonstration of all, Operation Little Switch.

On 9 April, the Sixth used 13 aircraft to airlift 597 combat-ready troops and 19,700 pounds of equipment to the 40th Inf. Div. during a 40-minute exercise. A never-ending chain of aircraft picking up men and supplies and landing them in designated areas nearby took 160 lifts. The demonstration climaxed two and one-half days of training the troops which would be riding in the helicopters and loading and unloading them.

On 14 April, a more impressive demonstration was given before General Taylor and the senior combat commanders in Korea. Assault elements of an infantry company were moved from an assembly area to simulated tactical blocking positions. Within ten and one-half minutes, 125 troops were moved a distance of five miles by 16 H-19's. In less than 14 minutes, 24,000 pounds of food, fuel and ammunition (enough to sustain an infantry company for a full day of fighting) were moved by sling-loading beneath the bellies of the aircraft. Also demonstrated were internal loading techniques for the big whirlybirds, and the evacuation mission techniques which required only three minutes from ambulance to air lift.

So impressed by what he saw was General Taylor that he said afterward: "We have seen before us today not a toy, but a new weapon to which we will have to give a lot of thought and use wisely." The statement was significant to the old-time Cub pilots who could remember vividly the reactions of other days.

Meanwhile, the Sixth had been alerted on 12 April for its role in "Little Switch" which had been planned for 20 April. The following week was filled with a flurry of activity as the Sixth prepared its aircraft for its historical mission.

On 19 April, 18 helicopters left Chunchon for a new base of operations at Inchon. The pilots and crew chiefs carried with them enough personal gear to last them as long as it would take to complete the job. That afternoon, the aircraft were flown to a soggy rice paddy adjacent to Freedom Village near Munsan-ni, where a command post was set up for their operations. That night, a platoon of six choppers remained at the CP just in case the Reds changed their oscillating minds and decided to start the exchange of prisoners before the appointed time. By 0800 the next day, all 18 helicopters were on hand to begin "Little Switch", which was due to start at 0900 hours. At the appointed time, the first four litter patients to arrive at Freedom Village were unloaded from litter-bearing H-13's in the presence of General Mark W. Clark and Lt. Gen. Maxwell D. Taylor. The four patients included two Americans, a Canadian and a Turk who were rushed into the line of tents which made up Freedom Village and the 45th MASH. Within 30 minutes, they came out wearing GI hospital pajamas and robes and were loaded into the waiting H-19 which headed for the 121st Evac. Hosp. in Seoul. During the day, 60 flights were logged by the helicopters which carried 100 patients to the 121st US and the 36th ROK hospitals in Seoul.

The second day found 100 patients evacuated from the 45th MASH and the 5th ROK Surgical hospitals at Munsan-ni in 59 flights.

On the third day, an H-19 was dispatched into Panmunjom proper in answer to an emergency call to pick up four litter cases. The chopper arrived within 15 minutes of the call.

On 24 April, near-tragedy struck the Sixth. At 1115 hours, an H-19 loaded with six repatriated ROK's experienced engine failure which resulted in an emergency landing into a rice paddy only 30 seconds after takeoff from the 5th ROK MASH. Even though the aircraft sustained major damage, no one was injured. Other helicopter pilots witnessed the crash from Freedom Village. Within four minutes, another helicopter had landed nearby to take on the passengers for the flight to Seoul.

Throughout the six days of "Little Switch", more than 170 flying hours were logged by the 6th Transportation Helicopter Company with an average of 17 choppers in the air every day. Their evacuation of prisoners of war became a "first" in Army Aviation history which they hoped will never need to be repeated.

Even with the exchange of sick and wounded prisoners of war, there was still no peace in Korea. The Army Aviator's war continued on the three fronts of weather, terrain and the enemy.

On 15 May, the Sixth moved out against the terrain. The treacherous roads had proved a menace to Army rolling equipment. A great deal of time was lost in costly repairs on vehicles which travelled the rocky, twisting, mountain passes. The Helicopter Company took the offensive to show how this condition could be modified with the use of choppers. At 0800 hours, the Sixth began the movement of a complete ROKA Field Artillery Battalion in the X Corps area to a new position behind the front lines. Within two hours, the job

was completed and five days of hard travel had been eliminated. The helicopters moved 480 soldiers and 14,000
pounds of precious cargo (including the electronic fire direction apparatus) without mishap.

A mission never before accomplished by Army Aviation was
undertaken on 20 May by the Sixth when it supplied three infantry regiments on the line with food, fuel and ammunition
to sustain battle operations for a period of three days. "Operation Skyhook" began at 0820 hours in heavy rain squalls.
For seven rain-drenched hours, 14 helicopters made 150
round trips to and from nine drop sites located on the front
lines in the 25th Division area. More than 57 tons of supplies
were carried during this period, despite three hour-long in-
terruptions. On the second day, one of the helicopters was
diverted to evacuate six wounded UN soldiers in another
sector of Korea. And later, three more wounded were evacuated. Yet, by 1300 hours, the previous day's record had
been surpassed. By 1400 hours of 22 May, "Sky Hook" had
been accomplished. The understrength helicopter company
had hauled an astounding total of 622,684 pounds of supplies
in 1,486 relay flights from Division supply points to the front
lines. History had been made. And the commander of the
25th Inf. Div., Major General Williams, expressed his sat-
isfaction that "one company of Army helicopters can support
three MLR regiments".

"Little Switch" had provided the prelude to the peace. The
proposal for the exchange of sick and wounded prisoners of
war had been made on 22 February by General Mark W. Clark.
On 1 April, an exchange agreement with the Reds had been
signed, and the complete exchange of prisoners was effected
by 3 May. In the weeks following, the dickering between the
negotiators followed the pattern set by the Communists two
years before. Finally, on 9 June, staff officers of both sides
began working on the cease-fire line to be agreed upon. The
end seemed imminent.

On 14 June, the Reds launched the biggest offensive of more
than two years of patrol action when they drove ROK troops
back as much as eight miles along a 20-mile front in the
east-central sector, from Kumwha to the Pukhan River.
The weather helped to stabilize the line on the second day of
the Red offensive when heavy rains softened the roads and
sent flash floods swirling down the mountain ravines. Although the weather stopped the enemy forces and friendly
Air Force planes as well, Army Aviators continued their
missions through the rain and low clouds to report that the

Reds were shuttling artillery, supplies and fresh infantry troops toward their newly-occupied positions. Red infiltration units were reported as much as four miles behind the Allied main line.

With the clearing of Korean skies, Allied air power and the four ROK divisions which had borne the brunt of the Red attack fought back in an attempt to nullify the Red gains which had come at a time when the final cease-fire line was being negotiated. The air arm was bolstered with bombs and rockets to drop on the enemy. President Syngman Rhee ordered his troops to stand firm and die if necessary to stop the Chinese invaders. Most of the ground lost a month before was finally retaken by the ROK's to the extent of five and one-half miles on 16 July by a three-division attack. And on 24 July, substantially all truce terms were agreed upon.

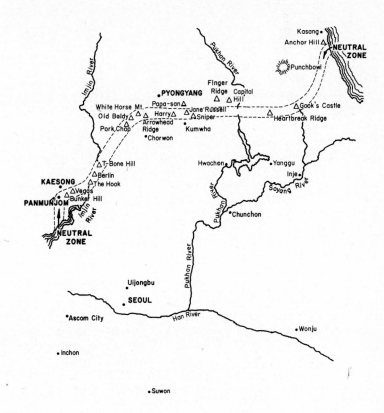

CEASE - FIRE

1953

In spite of threats to the truce which had arisen from the release by the ROK's of 25,000 North Korean anti-Communist prisoners and the opposition of Syngman Rhee to anything but complete victory for the Allies, the truce was signed at 2100 hours, 26 July 1953. The cease-fire was to be effective at 0900 hours, 27 July.

Army Aviation played its part to the very end of the war. Helicopters carried commanders along the new lines of the neutral zone to inspect the withdrawal of troops from both sides. Lt. Gen. Reuben Jenkins, commander of the US IX Corps, made a flight only 30 feet above the ground. The contrast of this flight was an anticlimax to others along the same route which had been made to the accompaniment of artillery dueling, anti-aircraft and small arms firing. Now the silence was disconcerting. And men of both sides were standing erect in the open for the first time in their combat tours of duty.

The truce created an emotional anticlimax for the Army Aviators, as well. The "sweat" of flying the front lines was eliminated insofar as the action of the Red enemy was concerned. But the two fronts of weather and terrain remained to plague them as long as they would stay on the peninsula.

During the last two months of the conflict, the 7th Inf. Div. aviation section airlifted more than four tons of fuses a distance of 50 miles over impassable roads in order to maintain heavy firepower against the attacking hordes of Reds. This airlift from a rear area supply depot to the Division's forward airstrip was credited with the failure of the enemy in their attacks on outposts of T-Bone, Pork Chop and Alligator Jaws. The entire airlift was performed by aircraft organic to the division.

And as a fitting climax to OPERATION GRASSHOPPER in Korea, the Army Aviators transported more than 5,000 Indian troops from an aircraft carrier at Inchon to the demilitarized zone. "Operation Byway" proved to be the largest movement of troops ever attempted by Army helicopter. The H-19's were used to place the Indians at their posts to police the cease-fire agreement which called for the questioning of prisoners of war as to whether they desired repatriation.

The war was over. But even with the ending of hostilities, the mysterious disappearance of Major Larry Loos on 18 February 1952 was never solved. But the prisoner of war exchanges during "Operation Big Switch" in August produced the solutions to other disappearances.

Lt. Conrad J. "Frenchy" Provencher of Lawrence, Massachusetts, appeared at Freedom Village on 31 August. The 190-pound Army Aviator weighed in at 155 pounds after his six months' imprisonment which had found him suffering frozen feet, diarrhea, piles, severe colds, worms and blood poisoning which raised great boils on his body. "Frenchy" was able to tell his "clank" story for the first time.

"It all started on February 19, 1952.

"At the time, I was flying a G-2 mission during which my observer, Private Bickle, was throwing out propaganda leaflets. Since the sun had already set, I was making my last pass over the front. I made a 100-degree turn to the south over the boot west of T-Bone Hill, then I immediately banked to the right when a 37-mm shell hit my engine. I was hit in the head and hands by shrapnel. The plexiglass windshield of the L-19 disintegrated into my face, arms and hands. The fire wall was blown out at the left hand side of the engine and the flames came shooting through the cockpit at me. I cut off the gasoline switches in the wing slots and headed the plane toward friendly lines. Then I couldn't see any more. I felt the ship wobble in the air and the controls softened in my hands as she approached a stall. I ordered Bickle to bail out. Before I could follow him, the plane went into a violent spin to the right. I pulled myself out of my seat and groped through the door. When I sensed myself clear of the aircraft, I tightened my grip to pull the D-ring of my parachute. But the tail section of the L-19 swiped me in the buttocks. I must have passed out. Free-falling through the cold air revived me a couple of seconds later so that I was able to pull the ripcord at about 800 feet above the ground. The chute opened with a jerk which almost separated my head from my body (at least it felt that way).

"While floating down those few hundred feet, I was aware that the Chinese were trying to machine-gun me. I was in a state of shock. When I hit the ground, I rolled, struck my head against a frozen furrow and sat, for I don't know how long, shaking my head to clear it of buzzing noises. When I came around, I noticed that the Reds were spraying in my direction with a machine gun. Dust was flying all around me and tracers were winking straight at me. The 'zzingg' of ricocheting bullets sounded just like they do in the movies. I got out of my chute harness in a hurry and dove between two furrows. I popped my head up once to see what was going on. The Chinese had me surrounded. The invitation of their burp guns and grenades was irresistible. I went with them.

"Later, I figured out that I had landed on Pokkae, a Chinese outpost west of T-Bone. I never did see Bickle again.

"Immediately after my capture, I was taken to a cave in this outpost. Several hours later, I was walked in the darkness for an hour and a half to another cave where I was interrogated for the first time. From here, I was walked for another two hours to a third cave where I spent the remaining hours of the night and all of the following day. On the night of the 20th, I was put into a jeep and driven to a point I would estimate to be some 40 miles behind the lines. At a combination Chinese Army Headquarters and initial interrogation point, I received medical treatment in the form of sulfa powder every other day. The medication was sulfa of the same type the Americans left in China after World War II. This cleared up my head, face and hand wounds in less than three months. However, I was not able to get back the full use of my left hand for another two or three months. Sitting comfortably also became a problem, since my pubic bone had apparently been cracked when the tail assembly of the L-19 had hit me after my jump.

"I can't complain about treatment during interrogation. It wasn't pleasant, but I was never attacked. I was questioned daily for two months and five days, one to three times a day in periods lasting anywhere from one to four hours. During the interrogation sessions, I was threatened repeatedly and applied with what the newspapers have called 'brain washing' techniques. I was never harmed physically, however, and only once, outside of the course of interrogation, was I threatened with shooting.

"The first three months I ate the same food the Chinese got. It was a far cry from the approved diet of a GI mess, but I got used to it and rather missed it, as a matter of fact, when it turned out to be better than the food I was later served in a prisoner of war camp to which I was taken deeper into North Korea.

"I was moved from the Army Center on 30 March to a place we called Mine Camp. We believed this place to be located some 30 to 50 miles east of Pyongyang. I spent 17 days here getting the last of the interrogation treatment from the Chinese, who apparently gave up on me since I was moved north to Pyokton. In five days I was moved again to a POW camp at Obul, about ten miles northeast of Pyokton and an hour's walk from the Yalu.

"In the POW camp, the potato became the mainstay of a monotonous diet. Previously, millet, rice and sorghum had been the regular fare. Once a week, usually on Sunday, we had a good amount of pork, usually two pork pies prepared by our own cooks. During the week we were served fish or pork fat occasionally. The fish was edible, but the pork fat could be stomached by only the hardiest among us. Cabbage was the main vegetable besides potatoes. Often, a mixture of the two was served. Just before the signing of the truce and immediately thereafter, the food improved to such an extent that we ate meals of Stateside artistry.

"The prison compound to which I was assigned contained 30 men. In our valley there were six compounds, the largest holding about 75 men. The population of the camp totalled slightly more than 200 prisoners. The camp was made up of flying personnel and airmen for the most part, plus a few infantry officers who were segregated from the flyboys, and also the 'bad boys' from other camps who were scattered among us. Here I might mention that even after the signing of the truce, the Chinese continued their practice of taking prisoners out of their compounds for purposes of interrogation. I myself was taken out for questioning on 13 August. This interrogation lasted six hours. The Chinese threatened to keep me in the camp longer because I had not given them the information they desired. They threatened to hold up my repatriation until the last if I did not open up. Other prisoners of war who were taken out reacted as I did to the questioning. They either answered with a lot of gibberish that didn't mean anything, or they reminded the Chinese that since the Armistice had been signed, they had no right to continue interrogation.

"During the first week of August, several of our compounds were combined into one group of 150 men. We were moved into a different camp site which we considered far superior to our previous prison. The reason for this action by the Chinese we guessed to be the fact that the Red Cross was visiting several camps and the Chinese expected them to come to ours also. However, the Red Cross inspectors never did get to our camp, though material sent by them reached us during the second week in August. On the 18th, two days after we received the Red Cross packages, we began our trek south by truck. We were first driven to Mampo (I believe), and from there we were loaded into cattle cars. many of which still contained cattle droppings, for a three-day train ride to Kaesong.

"The Chinese knew I was an Army Aviator because they were the ones who had shot me down and they captured me with my parachute very much in evidence. I personally believe that having been an Army Aviator helped me more than it hindered me during my interrogation because I was able to convince them that I could not be familiar with our front line positions, the strength of our troops on the outposts, and the dispositions of the various regiments, battalions and troops. They crossed me up once during interrogation by asking how I knew where the front lines were situated in order to perform my mission if I had not been briefed as to disposition of troops. I countered with the fact that the front lines could easily be recognized from the air because on our side of the lines we had well-travelled roads leading to friendly positions, whereas the roads on their side were not noticeably used. "

EPILOGUE

From the first operations of the 24th Inf. Div. aviation section in Korea during the first week of July 1950 to the time the last shot was fired on 26 July 1953, Army Aviation played a role on the Korean stage which was as versatile as it was dynamic. All of the elements of the vicious, bloody battles which made the struggle the important chapter that it became in the history of military operations were portrayed by the actors on the aviation stage.

Their record speaks for them. And their accomplishments are far and away out of proportion to the small numbers of Army Aviators at any one time who were called upon for sacrifice. They flew more than 500,000 hours on that beleaguered peninsula, a handful at a time. They undertook more than 140,000 combat missions, a handful at a time. About 40 of their aircraft were lost to enemy fire. Fifteen pilots gave up their lives, while unnumbered others became casualties of war. By the end of the campaigns, almost 20,000 UN sick and wounded were evacuated by helicopter from the battlefield, in addition to the thousands who were rescued from flood areas and from inaccessible terrain. According to the best official records, 1,027 Army pilots saw service in Korea. Of these, only six were listed as missing in action. Two of them were returned during the prisoner exchanges.

Assistant Secretary of the Army Earl D. Johnson has said that "There are unlimited tales of heroism to be found among the men who flew at low altitude week after week over enemy lines, their lives and their work linked closely to the savage ground fighting immediately beneath them." Some of these stories have been included in this volume. That there are many more, there is no doubt in the mind of the author who has found an extreme reticence among Army Aviators in recounting their experiences. But the many "firsts" which Army Aviation chalked up in Korea speak for themselves.

1. The first use of the helicopter by the Army to assist ground operations.

2. First establishment of an Army air transportation organization for administrative flying of Army headquarters staff in an active combat theater.

3. First air-drop of flame throwers to troops fighting on the line.

4. First feature-length films on Army Aviation to be made in an active combat theater.

5. First shore-to-ship evacuation of wounded by Army helicopter.

6. First use of multi-passenger Army aircraft in a combat theater.

7. First use of multi-engine Army aircraft in a combat theater.

8. First assignment of an Army Aviator to act as public information officer for Army Aviation in a field unit.

9. First use of Army helicopters in a mass exchange of prisoners of war.

10. First use of radar in Army aircraft operations in a combat theater.

THE NEW LOOK *of the Army is mobility which is demonstrated by the H-25. This aircraft can haul 5 men plus pilot.* (U. S. Army Photo)

As Eighth Army Headquarters made up its summary of the war, it revealed that one Navy Cross, 723 Distinguished-Flying Crosses, and 8,483 Air Medals had been awarded to Army Aviators. Among the awards of other decorations such as the Legion of Merit, Silver Star, Bronze Star and Purple Heart, are those to hundreds of Army Aviators whose exact numbers have not been determined.

This, then, was OPERATION GRASSHOPPER. At its climax, Army Aviation was able to prove its versatility as a valuable adjunct to the ground forces. The success of their missions on the fighting front is unquestioned. Their future role as a partner in the Army team is assured. For the "new look" in the Army stresses mobility. And Army Aviation has proved itself equal to the task.

And even though the battlefield of Korea has provided the classroom and the proving ground for Army Aviation, only history can provide its glory.

CHRONOLOGY

June 1950

  25 - Korean war breaks out
  28 - Seoul falls to the Reds for the first time
     - Pentagon begins the recall of Reserve and National Guard Army Aviators

July 1950

   1 - First Army Aviators leave Japan for Korea
   3 - 24th Inf. Div. Aviation section leaves for Korea
   4 - First Army Aviation mission is flown against the enemy
   7 - Lt. A. O. Munson becomes the first Army Aviation casualty
  10 - 8th Army aviation section arrives in Korea
     - 25th Inf. Div. aviation section flies to Korea
  12 - Capt. A. P. Bolding and Lt. Robert Adams shot down
  14 - Lt. Woodrow Brown has three feet of his left wing shot off
  17 - 1st Cav. Div. aviation section joins the battle
  18 - 24th Inf. Div. aviation section makes its first withdrawal during the battle for Taejon
  19 - Lt. John Dusell shot down by Yak-9's
  28 - 25th Division planes resupply units cut off near Sangju
  29 - General Walker posts "stand or die" order for the Pusan Perimeter

August 1950

   2 - 1st Marine Division lands in Korea
   8 - 2nd Inf. Div. aviation section joins the line
     - First Psychological Warfare leaflets dropped by Army light planes
  25 - Maj. Gen. William F. Dean, 24th Inf. Div. commander, is captured by the Reds

September 1950

  2 - Capt. W. L. Armstrong and Lt. W. A. Baugh fly the first air mission for the 2nd Division near the Naktong River

15 - X Corps lands at Inchon for "Operation Chromite"

16 - Capt. Charles Keleman makes a takeoff from carrier "Badoeng Straits" for Kimpo; must return to carrier

18 - Lt. LaMonne is the first Army Aviator to parachute to safety

    - General Walker flies 75 miles behind enemy lines in an L-5

19 - Lt. Richard Peterson shot down by ground fire

26 - 8th Army and X Corps link up near Suwon

29 - Seoul liberated by the UN

October 1950

  1 - EUSAK announces all organized resistance ended in South Korea

    - Army announces ear-marking of more than $42 million for purchases of new light planes

    - Thirty-day refresher course for recalled reserve pilots is begun at Fort Sill

10 - I ROK Corps captures Wonsan

18 - Lt. John Stanton killed in L-17 after colliding with friendly fighter aircraft

19 - Pyongyang falls to UN forces

20 - 187th RCT dropped near Anju

26 - ROKA troops reach the Yalu

November 1950

  1 - 124th Chinese Communist Division engaged by UN forces

11 - Turkish Brigade aviation section arrives with L-18's

20 - 7th US Inf. Div. reaches the Yalu

24 - 8th Army jumps off in attack against the Chinese

26 - CCF attack at Chosin Reservoir and begin steamrolling southward; UN forces withdraw

    - Lt. Robert A. Michelson evacuates wounded in his L-5 and resupplies units at Hagaru-ri

December 1950

    - 7th Division flyers assist in evacuation to Hungnam

11 - UN troops break out of the Chosin Reservoir trap
23 - General Walker killed in jeep accident
24 - X Corps evacuated from Hungnam
27 - Lt. Gen. Matthew B. Ridgway assumes command of EUSAK
 - Captain Marcus L. Sullivan flies the first Army helicopter at Ascom City

January 1951

1 - CCF forces drive southward in concentrated attack
3 - Captain Albert C. Sebourn makes first helicopter evacuation of wounded in Seoul area
4 - Seoul falls to the Reds for the second time
24 - CCF offensive stalled

February 1951

1 - UN Assembly brands Red China an "aggressor"
16 - 2nd Division fights the Reds in the Wonju-Chipyong-ni area; Army Aviation section credited with 5,000 enemy casualties
 - First Cessna L-19 arrives in Korea
20 - Captain John Olihovik rescues a Navy pilot shot down in no-man's land

March 1951

14 - Seoul retaken by UN troops
22 - 8th Army Flight Detachment formed
23 - 187th RCT dropped at Munsan-ni in "Operation Tomahawk" as General Ridgway observes from an L-5

April 1951

13 - 2nd Inf. Div. pilots pioneer night flying artillery missions
14 - General James A. Van Fleet assumes command of EUSAK
24 - 24th Division aviation section overrun by Reds

May 1951

16 - "May Massacre" begins. Air OP credited with 60 per cent of the enemy casualties
17 - 2nd Division stops Reds, killing 10,000 daily
23 - 2nd Division counterattacks
30 - Reds thrown behind the 38th Parallel

June 1951

23 - UN Soviet Delegate Jacob A. Malik proposes cease-fire in Korea

July 1951

10 - First cease-fire conference held at Kaesong

August 1951

23 - Reds break off talks, charging violation of the neutral zone by UN aircraft

September 1951

- Captain Ashby Snow goes Red-hunting with a carbine in his L-19
7 - Lt. Gene Rughlander crashes in his helicopter and saves the life of a wounded soldier
18 - 2nd Division pilots resupply an infantry battalion near Yanggu

October 1951

- Heartbreak Ridge
10 - Captain Robert R. Harding makes a night flight with plasma
- Captain George B. Daniels pioneers air-drop of flame throwers to hard-pressed troops
- Lt. Ed Zeigler delivers flame throwers by helicopter
25 - Truce negotiations resume after being moved to Panmunjom
27 - 7th Division aviation section is awarded the Distinguished Unit Citation for its evacuation of sick and wounded during the Chosin Reservoir operations in 1950

November 1951

3 - Lt. Robert A. Michelson and Lt. Col. Joseph D. O'Hanlon fly a night evacuation mission

December 1951

- Stateside magazines carry the account of the killing of two NK soldiers by a C-ration box dropped out of the plane of Major Robert L. Boatright during a resupply mission at Heartbreak

22 - First L-20 DeHavilland Beaver arrives in Korea
28 - Lt. Marvin K. Goulding parachutes to safety from
     his burning L-19
   - Lt. James F. Reed sinks a tank

January 1952

   - 40th Inf. Div. replaces the 1st Cav. Div.
   - "Van Fleet Weather" legend is firmly established
12 - Army Aviation joins the Navy for shore-to-ship
     evacuation of wounded
24 - Truce talks stalemated on Red demands for forcible
     repatriation of prisoners of war

February 1952

18 - Major Larry Loos listed as missing in action
24 - Captain Charles N. Posz lands safely after 12 square
     feet of his L-19's right wing is shot off

March 1952

 1 - Posz helps to rescue crews of two UN tanks disabled
     by enemy mines
 3 - First class of ROK Army Aviators reports for train-
     ing
22 - "Dragon Flight" celebrates its first anniversary

April 1952

   - "Operation Flicker" initiated
   - Captain William R. Chaires equips his L-19 with a
     home-made rig for DDT spraying
28 - General Mark W. Clark appointed to replace Ridgway
     as Far East Commander

May 1952

 4 - First class of ROK Army Aviators is graduated at
     Kwangju
 9 - General Clark flies with "Dragon Flight" on his first
     inspection tour of Korea

June 1952

 6 - Army Aviators celebrate their tenth anniversary
21 - Major William P. Hunt and Lt. Marvin S. Murphy
     are killed while observing for an infantry unit in the

attack.   Both are recommended for the Congressional Medal of Honor

July 1952

3 - Hunt-Murphy Field dedicated at Chipori by the 7th Division
- Lt. William G. Phillips clobbers the first Beaver in Korea
6 - Lt. Gen. "Iron Mike" O'Daniel is designated "Honorary Army Aviator"
- Lt. William M. Bogert flies his L-19 headon into a shell, make unknown

August 1952

- Army helicopters evacuate troops and civilians stranded by flood waters
- Army Aviation unshackled from Ordnance Corps and turned over to Transportation Corps for maintenance

September 1952

- "Dragon Flight" awarded the Meritorious Unit Citation
14 - Columbia Studios sends a five-man crew to film "Mission Over Korea"

October 1952

6 - Medical Service Corps officers begin helicopter training at Fort Sill
8 - UN calls indefinite recess of truce talks
27 - Filming of "Mission Over Korea" completed

November 1952

2 - L-19 piloted by Lt. Clyde P. Johnson hit by ack-ack.   Johnson bailed out after determining that his observer had been killed
- Lt. Sam Dugan and observer successfully bail out of their burning L-19.   Dugan had replaced Johnson

December 1952

1 - L-23 reaches Korea
2 - President-elect Eisenhower begins a three-day visit

in Korea, where he is flown by Colonel Swenson in an L-19

3 - ROKA pilot bugs out with L-19 to Nam Il
- Cardinal Spellman spends his second Christmas with the troops in Korea

January 1953

16 - General Order #9 establishes The Army Aviation School at Fort Sill, Oklahoma
23 - Lt. Gen. Maxwell D. Taylor named to relieve retiring Van Fleet as EUSAK commander

February 1953

1 - Major Raymond R. Evers experiments with "round-the-clock" Army Aviation observation
5 - 6th Helicopter Transportation Company arrives at Inchon
16 - Captain Melvin Rorick flies "George" in "Operation Sucker"
19 - Lt. Conrad J. Provencher shot down near T-Bone and is listed MIA

March 1953

26 - Lt. Landon Reid shot down and captured by the Reds
30 - Reds announce agreement to exchange all prisoners on a voluntary basis

April 1953

1 - General Mark Clark agrees to resume truce negotiations provided quick agreement is reached on sick and wounded exchange
- Agreement signed for exchange of sick and wounded in "Operation Little Switch"
20 - "Little Switch" begins
26 - 6th HTC completes its part in "Little Switch"

May 1953

3 - "Little Switch" is completed

June 1953

8 - Agreement on POW issues remain the only cease-fire issues
9 - Staff officers start drafting the final cease-fire line

14 - Reds launch biggest offensive in more than two years
18 - Some 25,000 North Korean POW's break out of ROK prison camps under orders of Rhee
20 - Truce talks recessed

July 1953

10 - Truce talks resumed
16 - ROK's open three-division attack to straighten the central front bulge made by the Reds' June 14 attack
24 - All truce terms agreed to
26 - Truce signed at 2100 hours
27 - Cease-fire in effect at 0900 hours

August 1953

31 - Lt. Provencher exchanged during "Operation Big Switch"

THE ARMY AVIATOR'S ALBUM

VOCABULARY

BABY-SAN - Korean infant
BATTLE RATTLE - battle fatigue
BIG "R" - rotation to Stateside duty
BOONDOCKS - a very remote area
BUG-OUT - evacuate in a hurry
BUG-OUT BAG - small suitcase packed with bare essentials to be carried in the event of a bug-out
BURLAPPER - Regular Army man
CARPET-BAGGER - Regular Army man
CHOGIE - plod along
CHOP CHOP - chow, food; also, with speed
CHOPPER - helicopter
CHOTA - good!, expression of approval
CLANKS - battle fatigue, nerves
CLANK STORY - war story
CLOBBERED - cracked up, destroyed; also drunk
CLUNKER - junky piece of machinery, viz., aircraft or vehicle
CONSTIPATION - affectionate name for the Navy's hospital ship, the USS Consolation
DAI JOBI - Okay
DICK - meaningless (often used in the phrase: "That doesn't mean "dick")
DOG FACE - Infantryman
EGG BEATER - helicopter
EUSAK - Eighth United States Army Korea
FLYBOY - applied to Army Aviators as a term of endearment or scorn
GEISHA HOUSE QUEENS - abortive term for GHQ personnel (general headquarters in Tokyo)
GOOK - term applied to foreigners in the Far East
GRANITE MOUNTAIN - emergency leave to the U. S.
GRAVEL AGITATORS - Infantrymen
GRENADE SIX - code name for General Ridgway
HELL FIRE - v.t., proximity fuse
HONCHO - boss, top man
HONEY BUCCANEER - Korean septic tank cleaner
HOT SPOT - run-up position for aircraft, located near the

beginning of the runway

HUBBA HUBBA - speedily

ICHIBAN - excellent, number one

IDIOT SHIP - helicopter

IDIOT STICKS - crossed-rifles insignia of the Infantry

INDIGNANT PERSONNEL - corruption of "indigenous" personnel, South Koreans employed by the Army

JAPANESE LAUNDRY COMPANY - abortive term for JLC, Japan Logistical Command

KCOMZ - Korea Communications Zone (US Army)

KMAG - Korea Military Advisory Group (US Army)

KIMCHI - a Korean food delicacy which evokes nauseous after-smells (mixture of pickled vegetables)

KIMCHI SIX - unofficial code name for President Syngman Rhee

KNOCKED - to have it made, to have a good deal

LITTLE "R" - rotation from combat duty to rear area

MAMA-SAN - elderly Korean female

MASH - mobile army surgical hospital

MIDA-MIDA - look for, look at

MIKE PETER - military policeman

MILE HIGH CLUB - exclusive club for flying lovers

MLR - main line of resistance

MOOSE - Korean female, usually young

MPC - armed forces currency, Military Payment Certificates

MSR - main supply route

NEVER HOTCHI - won't do, no good

NO SWEAT - easy, simple

NOD FOR THE SOD - cleared to land the aircraft

NOSE BLEED - code name for the 46th OLAM

NOSE DIVE - code name for the 47th OLAM

NUMBER ONE - the best

NUMBER TEN - the worst

OLAM - Ordnance Light Aviation Maintenance Company

OPERATION FREEZE-OUT - designed to deprive Reds of shelter

OPERATION RELAX - rest leave in Tokyo

OUT THE KAZOO - an over-abundance

PAPA-SAN - elderly Korean male

POOP - official information

RAT RACE - group of planes carrying visiting brass on inspection tour

REFINED, HISSING, SLURPING SOUND - Japanese version of the GI wolf whistle

R & R - rest and recuperation leave

RING-KNOCKER - West Point graduate

ROK - Republic of Korea

ROKA - Republic of Korea Army
RUGGED - extraordinarily tough
SACK - bed or sleeping bag
SCOTCH SIX - code name for General Van Fleet
SCROUNGE - achieve by trade or surreptitious fingering
SEXY - real gone
SHORT-TIMER - one having little time left to serve in Korea
SNOCKERED - inebriated
STRING BEAN SIX - unofficial code name for General Clark
STUFFED CLOUDS - mountains obscured by clouds or fog
SUITCASE DRILL - practice packing for return to States
SUKOSHI - little, very small
SWEAT - strain, worry
TAKUSAN - large
TESTO-TESTO - give it a try
THREE FEET IN THE GREEN - wheels of the L-17 or L-23
   down and locked, ready to land
TRACTOR-TYPE AIRCRAFT - propeller-driven
TRUMAN'S ISLAND - the United States, home
VAN FLEET WEATHER - poor flying weather, with marginal
   ceiling and visibility
VHF - very high frequency radio
VIP - very important person
WHIRLYBIRD - helicopter

ALBUM

Experiences have a way of eluding memory. To preserve them, many aviators kept diaries. Some relied on a carefully-kept 201 file. Others clicked the shutters of cameras which became as much a part of their personal equipment as a cigarette lighter.

In the pages that follow are preserved one man's record of the war in pictures, which made up the language of the small world in which the aviator lived during his stay in the Land of the Morning Calm.

Field Marshal Earl Alexander (left), Great Britain's Defense Minister, accompanied by General James A. Van Fleet, Commanding General, Eighth U.S. Army, makes an aerial inspection of the 45th U. S. Infantry Division's Iron Triangle battlefield near Chorwon, Korea, on 16 June 1952.

Debbie Reynolds, of motion picture fame, preparing to board a DeHavilland L-20A at Dragon Flight Base in Seoul, Korea, after a personal appearance in 1952.

1st Lt. Melvin K. Goulding, Army Pilot (Austin, Texas), became a member of the Caterpillar Club when he bailed out of his blazing L-19A over North Korea, after being hit by enemy ground fire.

Helicopter evacuation of a wounded soldier somewhere along the active front in 1952. The use of helicopters for this work did much to reduce appreciably the number of dead which would otherwise have been encountered.

L-19A completely destroyed during severe weather flying. Continued operations during the storms of the Korean winter accounted for a surprisingly small number of accidents.

*In some instances it has taken the loss of a plane and pilot to prove
to a ground commander that atmospheric conditions, as well as those
of terrain, are those which dictate the situation of an airstrip from
which flight operations can be continued in safety.*

*Another photo of operational weather conditions in Korea. Low
ceilings and poor visibility changed only the conditions of a flight, not
the fact of it. This photo was taken at the "Racetrack" near Seoul,
Korea, in February of 1952.*

Rugged terrain was one of the foremost obstacles to Army Aviation in Korea. This photo is an excellent example of the terrain throughout the peninsula. This L-19A is operating with the 2nd Infantry Division.

Taken from the rear seat of an L-19A this photo clearly indicates the "Punch Bowl" northwest of Inje, Korea. This shot is taken from the eastern edge looking west across this area.

An aerial view of the K-37 Airstrip located in the vicinity of Taegu, Korea, on 15 March 1952. K-37 was one of the better Korean airfields in spite of its rather crude appearance.

Evidence of the difficulties involved with even daily servicing of aircraft is seen at this refueling point at the 3rd Infantry Division airstrip.

Servicing problems are readily apparent here where the lack of many of the necessities and hangar facilities indicate only the barest essentials are available.

The first DeHavilland Beaver L-20A delivered to Korea, shortly after its arrival. Notice the auxiliary fuel tank secured to the belly of the fuselage. This plane was particularly adapted to this country and immediately won wide acceptance.

A Piper L-4J preparing to leave on a liaison mission. This road is on the outskirts of Inchon, and is being used by the 7th Division Air Section as a landing field.

An L-19A of the Republic of Korea Army used in the program for training ROK soldiers to become Korean Army Aviators. The background in this photo indicates it was almost as tough to learn to fly as it was to operate with the forward troops, insofar as terrain is concerned.

A Beech L-23A attached to HQ, 8th Army, at the Army A-2 airstrip on 1 November 1953. (Charles N. Trask)

A North American L-17C attached to the 2nd Engineer Construction Group at the K-16 Air Force Base in Seoul, on 21 September 1953. (Charles N. Trask)

A Bell H-13D at the A-33 Army air strip at Ascom City, Korea, on 9 November 1953. (Charles N. Trask)

A Sikorsky H-19C at the K-16 Air Force Base, Seoul, on 6 December 1953. (Charles N. Trask)

A *DeHavilland Beaver L-20A of the 8020th AU, United Nations Command, Military Armistice Commission, at K-16 Air Force Base, Seoul, on 6 December 1953. (Charles N. Trask)*

A *Cessna Bird Dog L-19A-CE of the 5th FA Group at the A-38 Army air strip near Hahuiyak, Korea, on 21 August 1953. (Charles N. Trask)*

A Cessna OE-1 of the Marine Corps at K-16 Air Force Base, Seoul, on 13 January 1954. (Charles N. Trask)

A Sikorsky HO5S-1 of the Marine Corps at K-16 Air Force Base, Seoul, on 2 July 1954. (Charles N. Trask)

A Sikorsky HRS-2 of the Marine Corps at K-16 Air Force Base, Seoul, on 2 July 1954. (Charles N. Trask)

A Stinson L-5-VW of the Air Force at K-16 Air Force Base, Seoul, on 28 August 1953. (Charles N. Trask)

A DeHavilland Beaver L-20A of the Air Force at K-16 Air Force Base, Seoul, on 6 August 1953. (Charles N. Trask)

A Cessna Bird Dog L-19A-CE of the ROK Army at A-38 Army air strip near Hahiuyok, Korea, on 22 August 1953. (Charles N. Trask)

A Cessna L-19A-CE of the U. S. Army carrying the wing insignia of the ROK. Probably this photo was taken during the repainting of the plane before transfer to the ROK Army. Actually, if the plane were to be flown in this insignia it would be in violation of the Geneva Convention which stated that an airplane shall carry the markings of one country only. This photo was taken at the A-33 Army air strip at Ascom City, on 9 November 1953. (Charles N. Trask)

An Aero Commander 520 of the ROK Air Force. This plane was not a transferred airplane from the U. S. Air Force but was purchased by the ROK second hand. This plane was originally licensed in the U. S. as N2617B. At least three airplanes of this model were assigned to the ROK; numbers 501, 502, and 503 (shown) are known to exist. This photo was taken at K-16 Air Force Base, Seoul, on 4 April 1954. (Charles N. Trask)

A Piper L-4J of the ROK Army still bears the same serial number it was assigned by the USAAF way back in '45 — 45-5082. This photo was taken at "Taegu South" [K-37], on 31 January 1951. (B. C. Reed)

A Stinson L-5 (modification unknown) of the ROK Air Force at K-46 Air Force Base, Wonju, on 15 August 1953. (Charles N. Trask)

The only Bird Dog (L-19A-CE) obtained by the British. This plane still bears the original Army serial number (51-4754). This photo, taken at K-16 Air Force Base, Seoul, on 13 November 1953, clearly shows this original serial number on both the fin and wing. (Charles N. Trask)

An Auster Mk. 6 of the Royal Air Force (Serial Number VF547 identifies it as English) at K-16 Air Force Base, Seoul, on 2 July 1954. (Charles N. Trask)

An Auster Mk. 7 of the Royal Air Force (Serial Number WE591 identi-
fies it as English) at K-16 Air Force Base, Seoul, on 21 September 1953.
Notice the difference in the markings on this airplane and the Auster
Mk. 6 shown previously. Both are airplanes of the Royal Air Force
and there is no known reason for this markings difference. (Charles
N. Trask)

This Turkish Air Force Piper "Cub" (L-18B) was practically new at
the time this photo was taken (7 February 1951) though it carried a
U. S. Air Force Serial Number. This airplane was photographed at
the Suwon (K-13) air strip. (B. C. Reed)

INDEX

UNITS

PERSONALITIES

214

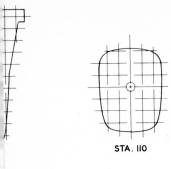

STA. 110

STA.205

STA. 228

RADIO EQUIPMENT

BC 1335 RADIO AND TRANSMITTER

ARC T-11A L.F. TRANSMITTER

ARC T-13 V.H.F. TRANSMITTER

ARC R-11A L.F. RECEIVER

ARC R-19 V.H.F. RECEIVER

BC 1335 TRANSMITTER & RADIO
OMITTED ON SERIALS 23100
THRU 23119

ABOVE EQUIPMENT IS TYPICAL.
CONSIDERABLE VARIATION MAY
OCCUR IN THE FIELD.

NS

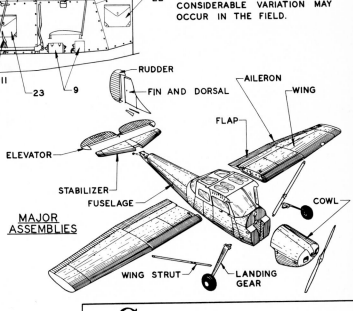

RUDDER

FIN AND DORSAL

AILERON

WING

FLAP

ELEVATOR

STABILIZER

FUSELAGE

COWL

MAJOR
ASSEMBLIES

WING STRUT

LANDING
GEAR

RE

1950
1951
1952
1953
1954

Cessna L-19A
"BIRD DOG"

THE ROBERT R. LONGO CO, INC.

DRAWN BY: JOHN J. ZAWISKI

DATE: MARCH, 1958

SHEET 3 OF 3